A Treasury of Sacred Maxims

THE TREASURY SERIES IN
ISLAMIC THOUGHT AND CIVILISATION

I. *A Treasury of Ḥadīth*, Ibn Daqīq al-ʿĪd

II. *A Treasury of al-Ghazālī*, Mustafa Abu Sway

III. *A Treasury of Sacred Maxims*, Shahrul Hussain

IV. *A Treasury of Ibn Taymiyyah*, Mustapha Sheikh

V. *A Treasury of Rūmī*, Muhammad Isa Waley

VI. *A Treasury of Iqbal*, Abdur Rashid Siddiqui (Forthcoming)

Shahrul Hussain

كنوز من القواعد الفقهية

A Treasury of Sacred Maxims

KUBE
PUBLISHING

For…

FJ

A Treasury of Sacred Maxims

First published in England by
Kube Publishing Ltd
Markfield Conference Centre
Ratby Lane, Markfield
Leicestershire LE67 9SY
United Kingdom

TEL +44 (0)1530 249230
FAX +44 (0)1530 249656
WEBSITE www.kubepublishing.com
EMAIL info@kubepublishing.com

2nd impression 2021

CIP data for this book is available from the British Library.

ISBN 978-1-84774-096-0 casebound
ISBN 978-1-84774-108-0 ebook

Cover design Inspiral Design
Book design Imtiaze Ahmed
Arabic & English typesetting nqaddoura@hotmail.com
Printed by Elma Printing, Turkey

Contents

Transliteration Table

Arabic Consonants

Initial, unexpressed medial and final: ء ʾ

ا a	د d	ض ḍ	ك k
ب b	ذ dh	ط ṭ	ل l
ت t	ر r	ظ ẓ	م m
ث th	ز z	ع ʿ	ن n
ج j	س s	غ gh	هـ h
ح ḥ	ش sh	ف f	و w
خ kh	ص ṣ	ق q	ي y

With a *shaddah*, both medial and final consonants are doubled.

Vowels, diphthongs, etc.

Short:	a ـَ	ـِ i	ـُ u
Long:	ā ـَا	ـِي ī	ـُو ū
Diphthongs:		ـَوْ aw	
		ـَيْ ay	

Acknowledgments

‘*He who is not grateful to mankind is not grateful to Allah*’—It would be disingenuous for me to pretend that this work was a result of my sole endeavour. Therefore it behoves me to extend my deepest gratitude to those who helped me with this book. First and foremost, to my mother and father, for their encouragement and continuous support, and to my son Sami and daughter Omaymah for showing patience and understanding of my not spending more time with them. To all my teachers, all my friends, in particular Taj Ullah, and librarians, too numerous to mention by name, for their invaluable help, assistance and patience. To the scholars for their consultation, discussion and feedback, and to those who allowed me to use their personal libraries. Special thanks to my academic mentor, Dr Ataullah Siddiqui, for his continuous help and support, Dr Zahid Parvez, Principal of the Markfield Institute, for providing academic staff with the platform to engage in research and writing; and to Shaykh Mohammed Ziad Takleh for his help in hadith research and Arabic typing, as well as Abid Khan. My heartfelt thanks to Yahya Birt, this publication would not be possible without his help, for which I am eternally indebted to him. A very special thanks to the 'anonymous' reviewer(s) for their comments and annotations, in particular Shakira Choudhury. I would like to thank Usaama al-Azami, for his editorial support. My greatest expression of thanks is to my Lord, Whom I love so much and can never thank adequately. Any shortcomings or errors are mine, and I seek forgiveness and correction.

Shahrul Hussain
Sha'bān 1437

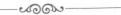

Introduction

All praises due to Allah, Who is unique in the majesty of His essence and the perfection of His attributes, and Who is free from blemishes and defects through the qualities that belong to His great Power. Peace and blessings be upon Muḥammad, the final Prophet of Allah and upon his Family and Companions.

A Brief Overview of Juristic Maxims

> These maxims are important and of tremendous benefit in jurisprudence. The rank and eminence of a jurist are directly proportional to his mastery of them. Knowledge of them highlights the splendour of fiqh and clarifies and reveals the methodology of fatwa. (al-Qarāfī)[1]

Juristic maxims (*al-qawā'id al-fiqhiyyah*) enjoy a special and privileged place in Islamic jurisprudence. It is a discipline which subtly combines a fusion of theoretical-cum-philosophical thought translated

1. Al-Qarāfī, Abū al-'Abbās Aḥmad ibn Idrīs al-Ṣanhājī, 1998. *Al-Furūq wa-Anwār al-Burūq fī Anwā' al-Furūq*, Beirut: Dār al-Kutub al-'Ilmiyyah, edited by Khalīl al-Manṣūr, vol. 1, p. 3.

into juristic dictums encompassing a multitude of jurisprudential rulings. This means that juristic maxims can be best understood as theoretical abstractions in the form of short epithetic statements that are expressive of major legal concepts affecting a vast part of law. Juristic maxims are in essence statements of principles extrapolated from a predominant governing theme with regards to a particular issue from the Qur'an, Sunnah and consensus. Many jurists have advanced various definitions of *qawā'id fiqhiyyah*. Their definition is influenced by two main approaches: first, the notion that juristic maxims apply to most but not all of the relevant cases. One of the proponents of this view is a prominent Ḥanafī jurist, Aḥmad ibn Muḥammad al-Ḥamawī, who describes juristic maxims in his commentary of Ibn Nujaym's *al-Ashbāh wa al-Naẓā'ir* as, 'a predominant, rather than a comprehensive rule that applies to most relevant cases, such that their ruling can be known from it.'[2] The second, which is the definition held by the majority of scholars, suggests that juristic maxims are comprehensive rules. Muḥammad ibn Muḥammad al-Maqqarī, a famous *Mālikī* jurist, defines it as, 'all the comprehensive rules that are more limited in scope than *uṣūl* (principles of Islamic jurisprudence), and general rational principles but more general than contractual rules and the

2. Al-Ḥamawī, Aḥmad ibn Muḥammad, 1985. *Ghamz al-'Uyūn al-Baṣā'ir fī Sharḥ al-Ashbāh wa al-Naẓā'ir*, Beirut: Dār al-Kutub al-'Ilmiyyah, vol. 1, p. 51.

particular jurisprudential parameters (*ḍawābiṭ*) that govern contracts.'[3] Al-Subkī's definition is simpler and more to the point, 'it is comprehensive matters that apply to numerous particular cases and by which their rulings can be understood.'[4] Both groups of scholars have strong proofs to substantiate their arguments whether it is a comprehensive coverage or majority coverage of jurisprudential issues. It is not my intention to provide an advanced critique of the merits of their claims. Instead my aim is to introduce the reader to the scholastic scope and thereby the application of juristic maxims. The main point is to give the reader a flavour of the significance and importance of juristic maxims and the role juristic maxims played in Islamic legal thought.

The reason why al-Qarāfī said that the rank and eminence of a jurist is directly proportional to his mastery of juristic maxims is because of the beneficial characteristic and far reaching scope of this discipline. *Qawā'id fiqhiyyah* regulates numerous widely dispersed issues and organises them in a single unit which enables the jurists to perceive the common feature that unite diverse particulars. Ibn Rajab says, 'for a jurist *qawā'id fiqhiyyah* organises scattered issues in a single unit, limits anomalies and

3. Al-Maqqari, Muḥammad ibn Muḥammad, nd. *Al-Qawā'id*, Makkah: Markaz Iḥyā' al-Turāth al-Islāmī, edited by Aḥmad ibn 'Abdullah ibn Ḥumayd, vol. 1, pp. 106-7.
4. Al-Subkī, Tāj al-Dīn 'Abd al-Wahhāb ibn Taqī al-Dīn al-Subkī, 1991. *Al-Ashbāh wa al-Naẓā'ir*, Beirut: Dār al-Kutub al-'Ilmiyyah), vol. 1, p. 11.

brings together widely separated issues.'[5] Mastering juristic maxims also reduces the need to memorise large amounts of legal rulings while at the same time enables jurists to be precise in their judgement. Al-Qarāfī says: 'One who attains mastery of *fiqh* by means of its legal maxims has no need to memorise most of the particular rulings since they come under the purview of the comprehensive principles. Moreover, the jurists will comprehend the unity and consistency in matters that others perceive as contradictory.'[6] Another key significance of juristic maxims is that it gives the jurist an idea of the level of flexibility allowable in tight and rigid cases. For example, what would happen in a case where a person was left with no alternative but to eat pork to survive? It simplifies the process of working out the result to a legal question.

The role juristic maxims played in Islamic legal thought can also be seen in some of its unique characteristics. The complicated and intricate theme is encapsulated in a short and easy to memorise phrase without losing the significance of having a wide ranging application. The maxims are precise with a subtle nuance reflecting the genius and penetrating intellect of the Muslim jurists. Mastering and using juristic maxims effectively requires encyclopaedic juristic expertise, vast discernment and intellectual maturity.

---

5. Ibn Rajab, 'Abd al-Raḥmān ibn Aḥmad, nd. *Al-Qawā'id*, Beirut: Dār al-Kutub al-'Ilmiyyah, vol. 1, p. 3.
6. Al-Qarāfī, *al-Furūq*, op. cit., vol. 1, p. 3.

The Legal Justification (*ḥujjiyah*) of Juristic Maxims

In general the legal justification (*ḥujjiyah*) of all juristic maxims comes from the Qur'an and Sunnah in one way or the other. But to understand this better I have divided juristic maxims into two types: the first are those types which are directly Qur'anic or look into precepts presented in a formulaic style. These are known as the five core maxims. These maxims are agreed upon and accepted by all jurists. For example, the maxim 'acts are judged by their goals and purposes' is based on the Prophetic tradition: 'Indeed all actions depend upon intention, and for every person is that which he intends.' (Bukhārī)

The second type is also based on the Qur'an and Sunnah but are subject to scholastic disagreement. This is because the connection between them and the textual references is not as strong and conclusive as the 'five core' maxims. For example, not all jurists agree on the maxim 'scholastic reasoning does not apply in the presence of a clear text', and its textual evidence is equally disputed amongst jurists.

The Five Core Maxims and Their Moral Philosophy

There are five core maxims and all other maxims are mostly subsidiaries to these five:

1. Acts are judged by their goals and purposes.
2. Harm is to be removed.
3. Customary usage is the determining factor.
4. Certainty is not overruled by doubt.
5. Hardship begets ease.

Morality and law work hand-in-hand. The law serves many purposes and functions in society. It helps in establishing standards, maintaining order, resolving disputes, protecting liberties and rights and much more. If we did not live in a structured society with other people, laws would not be necessary save spiritual law (*aḥkām al-ʿibādāt*). We would simply do as we please, with little regard for anything else. But this is not the natural way Allah designed human beings to live. Rather, humans are social creatures and need the company of other humans to function and live happy, fulfilling lives. In Islam, laws are designed to govern our conduct. Law in Islam is aimed at establishing fairness. This means that the law should recognise and protect certain basic individual rights and freedoms, such as liberty and equality. A part of this is to ensure that strong groups and individuals do not use their powerful positions in society to take unfair advantage of weaker individuals.

The idea of law is to govern the relationship on a societal level, to lay down boundaries and set rights and responsibilities. By observing this a person shows his servitude to his Creator, which is the ultimate purpose of human creation. Therefore, if the aim of law is to govern human relationships it means that it aims to bring about the optimal behaviour in people. This therefore means that Allah's law has a higher objective, which is an esoteric message in the form of moral philosophies. After all, the aim of law is to make humans behave in a responsible manner. Laws resemble morality because they are designed to control or alter our behaviour. But unlike rules of morality, laws are enforced by the courts with consequences for failure to implement decisions. This is where the role of *taqwā* or God-consciousness comes into play. In Islam, the law aims to inculcate in each individual the value of good behaviour, because the ultimate destination of humankind is to Allah. So a person should not be concerned with what the courts' will do but rather with what Allah will do. It is because of the strong connection between law and morality that after discussing the legal juristic understanding of each maxim I will attempt to shed light on the probable moral teachings of the maxim.

The Structure of this Book

Each maxim has three elements which will be discussed:

1. The intellectual coinage of the juristic maxim,
2. its legal justification (*ḥujjiyah*), and
3. its moral philosophy.

In all, I have selected forty maxims for this book. Each maxim will be explained, followed by examples of how it is applied in Islamic law. The *ḥujjiyah* of the maxim will be discussed and concluded by discussing the moral message the maxim gives. Below is an overview of the moral messages of the five core maxims:

1. **'Acts are judged by their goals and purposes.'** The moral message this maxim aims to teach is sincerity. Sincerity is the foundation of all acts of worship and worship is the principle purpose of human creation. Before anything, the primary goal of any Muslim should be to get his intention correct.
2. **'Harm is to be removed.'** The moral message this maxim aims to teach is outlining the principle code of conduct by which every Muslim should live his life, to wit, not to cause harm to others and he shall not be harmed.
3. **'Customary usage is the determining factor.'** The moral message this maxim aims to teach is one of tolerance and respect. No two people are the same and therefore there are bound to be different habits, practices and cultures. This is the greatness of Allah's power, how from one man and one woman humankind populated earth and celebrates a multitude of diverse cultures. Sharing a common ancestry means sharing and having a common love for all humanity.
4. **'Certainty is not overruled by doubt.'** The moral message this maxim aims to teach is that Muslims should have a good opinion (*ḥusn al-ẓann*) about everything. By doing this it will create a positive mindset in people to deal with the daily challenges of life.
5. **'Hardship begets ease.'** The moral message this maxim aims to teach is whenever dealing with others one should deal with them with

gentleness and ease, showing compassion and being thoughtful to the difficulties others may be facing.

In sum, *qawā'id fiqhiyyah* is a very important branch of Islamic jurisprudence because it provides a juristic frame of reference and outlook that illustrates the method to study and learn diverse and numerous aspects of *fiqh*, and it enables one to deduce solutions to newly arising issues that require Islamic legal interpretation.

The Historical Development of *al-Qawā'id al-Fiqhiyyah*

Much like other disciplines, juristic maxims are a result of cumulative progress which could not have been expected to take place at the formative stages of the development of *fiqh*. Evidence suggests that juristic maxims have their foundations from the time of the Companions. This is substantiated by narrations from Companions who expressed complicated juristic issues in the form of maxims, such as 'Umar ibn al-Khaṭṭāb coining the maxim, 'acceptance or rights are based on conditions', 'Alī ibn Abī Ṭālib saying: 'There is no liability on the one whoever distributes profit', and 'Abdullah ibn 'Abbās affirming, 'every matter in the Qur'an that uses the word "or" means choice'.[7] The development of juristic

7. Al-Nadwī, 'Alī Aḥmad, 1991. *Al-Qawā'id al-Fiqhiyyah*, Damascus: Dār al-Qalam, p. 82.

maxims continued during the formative period of Islamic jurisprudence and beyond. At different stages it received refinement and different emphases, and as a result of this different terminologies associated with it were used to describe this discipline such as *qawā'id fiqhiyyah*, *ḍawābiṭ fiqhiyyah*, and *ashbāh wa-naẓā'ir*.

Al-Qawā'id al-Fiqhiyyah and *al-Ḍawābiṭ al-Fiqhiyyah*

Kamāl ibn al-Humām, al-Nawawī, Ibn Rajab al-Ḥanbalī and others did not see a difference between *qawā'id fiqhiyyah* (juristic maxims) and *ḍawābiṭ fiqhiyyah* (jurisprudential principles) and regarded them as one and the same. The majority of scholars, however, regarded them as two different disciplines. Al-Zarkashī, Ibn al-Subkī, Ibn Nujaym and al-Suyūṭī point out the difference between the two. *Qawā'id fiqhiyyah* (juristic maxims) apply to detailed rulings across a wide range of *fiqh* chapters while *ḍawābiṭ fiqhiyyah* (jurisprudential principles) apply to a particular issue which cannot be applied to other issues. For example, the maxim 'harm is to be removed' covers many areas of jurisprudence while the *ḍabiṭ fiqhī* (jurisprudential principle) 'every animal that dies without being slaughtered is impure except for fish or locusts', has a particular application in terms of its relevance to a specific issue in Islamic law.

Al-Qawā'id al-Fiqhiyyah and *al-Ashbāh wa al-Naẓā'ir*

Another term is *ashbāh wa al-naẓā'ir* which roughly translated means 'similar and comparable issues'. Al-Suyūṭī best explains the difference between *qawā'id fiqhiyyah* and *ashbāh wa-naẓā'ir*: 'Certain issues have a different ruling than other cases which resemble them, because a particular consideration is given to a case. Issues are discussed which seem similar but have different rulings due to a disparity in their *'illah* (*ratio legis*). This is called *furūq*.'[8] The reality of the issue is that although there may be three names related to this discipline, most of the books combine all three topics in their writings with a particular focus on a particular topic.

The Pioneers of Juristic Maxims and their Works

It is related that the pioneers of this discipline were Ḥanafī scholars. Sufyān ibn Ṭāhir al-Dabbās put seventeen maxims together which were later added to by Abū al-Ḥasan al-Karkhī, who raised it to thirty nine. His book, *Uṣūl al-Karkhī*, not only contains this discipline, but it is also one of the early books on Ḥanafī *uṣūl al-fiqh*. It was the Shāfi'ī jurists who followed the Ḥanafīs who were then followed by the Ḥanbalīs and then the Mālikīs. Funnily enough,

8. Al-Suyūṭī, *al-Ashbāh*, op. cit., vol. 1, p. 31.

after many centuries it reverted back to Ḥanafī scholars who produced the largest work on this topic in contemporary times. Under the supervision of Aḥmad Cevdet Pasha, a group of Turkish Ḥanafīs attempted to codify Islamic law, calling it the *Mejelle-i-Ahkam 'Adliyye*. It should be noted that the *Mejelle* is not meant to be a juristic maxims book *per se* and therefore its layout and structure do not follow a similar systematic approach found in other books.

The names and contribution of the great pioneers of juristic maxims can be seen in the following list. I have listed some of the most important works on juristic maxims within each of the four schools of thought.

The Ḥanafī School

1. *Uṣūl al-Karkhī* by Abū al-Ḥasan al-Karkhī.
2. *Ta'sīs al-Naẓar* by Abū Zayd ibn 'Umar al-Dabbūsī.
3. *Al-Ashbāh wa al-Naẓā'ir* by Ibn Nujaym.
4. *Mejelle-i-Ahkam 'Adliyye.*
5. *Sharḥ al-Majallah* by Sālim Rustum Bāz.

The Mālikī School

1. *Anwār al-Burūq fī Anwā' al-Furūq* by Aḥmad ibn Idrīs al-Qarāfī.
2. *Īḍāḥ al-Masālik ilā Qawā'id al-Imām Mālik* by Abū al-'Abbās al-Wansharīsī.

3. *Al-Bāhir fī Ikhtiṣār al-Ashbāh wa al-Naẓā'ir* by Abū Zayd al-Fāsī.
4. *Manẓumāt al-Manhaj al-Muntakhab* by Abū al-Ḥasan al-Tujiyyī.

The Shāfi'ī School

1. *Qawā'id al-Aḥkām fī Maṣāliḥ al-Anām* by 'Izz ibn 'Abd al-Salām.
2. *Al-Ashbāh wa al-Naẓā'ir* by Muḥammad ibn 'Umar ibn al-Wakīl.
3. *Al-Majmū' al-Mudhhab fī Qawā'id al-Madhhab* by Khalīl ibn Kaykaldī.
4. *Al-Ashbāh wa al-Naẓā'ir* by Tāj al-Dīn al-Subkī.
5. *Kitāb al-Qawā'id* by Taqī al-Dīn al-Ḥisnī.
6. *Al-Manthūr fi al-Qawā'id* by Muḥammad ibn Bahādur al-Zarkashī.
7 *Al-Ashbāh wa al-Naẓā'ir fī Qawā'id wa Furū' Fiqh al-Shāfi'iyyah* by Jalāl al-Dīn 'Abd al-Raḥmān ibn Abī Bakr al-Suyūṭī.
8. *Manẓumāt al-Farā'id al-Bahiyyah fi al-Qawā'id al-Fiqhiyyah* by Abū Bakr al-Tihāmī al-Ḥusaynī al-Dimashqī.

The Ḥanbalī School

1. *Al-Qawā'id al-Nūrāniyyah* by Ibn Taymiyyah.
2. *Taqrīr al-Qawā'id wa-Taḥrīr al-Fawā'id* by Ibn Rajab al-Ḥanbalī.

3. *Al-Qawā'id al-Kulliyyah wa al-Ḍawābiṭ al-Fiqhiyyah* by Ibn 'Abd al-Hādī.
4. *Al-Qawā'id wa al-Uṣūl al-Jāmi'ah wa al-Furūq wa al-Taqāsīm al-Badī'ah al-Nāfi'ah* by 'Abd al-Raḥmān ibn Nāṣir al-Sa'dī.

Some Contemporary Works on Juristic Maxims

1. *Al-Qawā'id al-Fiqhiyyah* by 'Alī al-Nadwī.
2. *Al-Wajīz fī Īḍāḥ al-Qawā'id al-Kulliyyah* by Muḥammad Sidqī ibn Aḥmad al-Būrnū.
3. *Mawsu'at al-Qawā'id al-Fiqhiyyah* by Muḥammad Sidqī ibn Aḥmad al-Būrnū and Abū Ḥārith al-Ghazzī.
4. *Al-Madkhal al-Fiqhī al-'Āmm* by Muṣṭafā ibn Aḥmad al-Zarqā'.
5. *Al-Qawā'id al-Fiqhiyyah* by Ya'qūb al-Bāḥusayn.
6. *Al-Mumti' fī al-Qawā'id al-Fiqhiyyah* by Muslim ibn Muḥammad al-Dawsarī.

Just as I opened with a quotation from a master of the science of *qawā'id fiqhiyyah* I would like to conclude with a quotation from another master:

> *Indeed, the knowledge of* al-ashbāh wa al-naẓā'ir *is a great knowledge by which the reality of jurisprudence, its position, its source and its secrets are known. With it, one will be more prominent in understanding jurisprudence and having it at one's finger tips. It makes one able to relate and extract rulings*

and know the rulings of unwritten and new problems and realities that are in tandem with time. Therefore, some of our companions said that jurisprudence is the understanding of similarities. (Jalāl al-Dīn al-Suyūṭī)[9]

9. Al-Suyūṭī, Jalāl ad-Dīn 'Abd al-Rahmān ibn Abū Bakr, 1998. *Al-Ashbāh wa al-Naẓā'ir fī Qawā'id wa-Furū' Fiqh al-Shāfi'iyyah*, Beirut; Dār al-Kutub al-'Ilmiyyah, edited by Muḥammad Ḥasan Ismā'īl al-Shāfi'ī, vol. 1, p. 29.

I

Works are According to their Ultimate Ends

الأُمُورُ بِمَقَاصِدِها

Acts are Judged by their Goals and Purposes

The first of the five core maxims is *al-umūr bi-maqāṣidi-hā*. This maxim emphasises intention and purpose. As intention has a ubiquitous and focal presence in almost all aspects of law, it would be an understatement to say that its impact on Islamic law is prodigious. Intention is the soul of all physical, liturgical, spiritual and verbal worship. Whether the act of worship is accepted by Allah, or otherwise, depends on the validity of the intention. The textual evidence to underpin this maxim is the well-known hadith 'Indeed all actions depend upon intention, and for every person is that which he intends.' (Bukhārī)

Ibn al-Qayyim al-Jawziyyah describes this hadith as, 'two words under which lies a treasure-trove of knowledge'.[10] The laudation in terms of the significance of this hadith is stressed by many great classical scholars like Ibn Mahdi, Ibn al-Madīnī, Abū Dāwūd, al-Dāraquṭnī and others. These scholars regarded this hadith to represent a large share of knowledge, some saying it is a quarter and others a third. Imam Aḥmad ibn Ḥanbal maintained that the foundations of Islam can be encapsulated in three hadiths: as cited above, the hadith of 'Umar on intention which is related by Bukhārī; the hadith of 'Ā'ishah, 'Whoever, innovates in this affair of ours [i.e. Islam] that which is not from it then it is rejected' (Bukhārī and Muslim); and the hadith of Nu'man ibn Bashīr, 'The halal is clear and the haram is clear' (Bukhārī and Muslim). The weight of intention and its import in Muslim law can be seen by the descriptions afforded by al-Shāfi'ī and Abū Dāwūd. The former argues that, 'the hadith [of 'Umar afore-cited] is one third of all knowledge, and it is involved in seventy sections of jurisprudence.' Likewise, Abū Dāwūd declares that *fiqh* revolves around four hadiths. Like al-Shāfi'ī, he selects the hadith of 'Umar and Nu'man ibn Bashīr, and includes the hadith of Abū

10. Ibn al-Qayyim, Abū 'Abdullāh Muḥammad ibn Abī Bakr, *I'lām al-Muwaqqi'īn 'an Rabb al-'Ālamīn,* 1955. Cairo: Matba'ah al-Sa'adah, edited by Muḥammad Muḥyī al-Dīn 'Abd al-Ḥamīd, vol. 3, p. 123 (hereinafter cited as: Ibn al-Qayyim, *I'lām al-Muwaqqi'īn*).

Sa'īd al-Khudrī, 'There is no causing harm nor returning harm', (Tirmidhī, Ibn Majah and Mālik); and finally, the hadith of Abū Hurayrah 'Indeed Allah is pure, and only accepts that which is pure.' (Bukhārī and Muslim)

The reason why intention plays a major role in Islamic law is because it has three primary functions. It is used to distinguish acts of worship from ordinary daily or habitual acts. Secondly, the aim of intention is to distinguish one act of worship from another. This can best be illustrated by the following example: A person may give alms to the poor as well as give alms as zakat. When donating the money how can it be distinguished? Is it zakat, which is an obligatory Qur'anic precept to be observed, or was the bestowing of money a voluntary act of kindness to the less fortunate? The only way this can be differentiated is by assessing the intent behind the act. The place of intention for one who acts is his heart and not his tongue. For instance, this means that if a person who stands for prayer and inadvertently expresses the spoken intention of performing Ẓuhr prayer, while the intention in the heart is 'Aṣr prayer; then his prayer is 'Aṣr and not Ẓuhr. Thirdly, the purpose of intention is to attain spiritual reward (*thawāb*) and to seek the pleasure of Allah Most High. Therefore, to act without intention is free from spiritual reward.

Not all acts of worship require an intention, rather Muslim jurists maintain that for some acts of worship an intention is essential, while for others it is not, and some aspects of intention are the subject of scholastic debate. For example, it is agreed by the consensus of jurists that if a person abstains from eating, drinking and sexual gratification from dawn to dusk without having any intention of fasting, it does not count as a valid fast. However, for the call to prayer, intention is not a prerequisite. This means that if a person were to call the *adhān* without making any intention then that suffices provided that the time for prayer has commenced. This is because the objective of the *adhān* is to notify the people that the prayer time has started, so if a person makes the call to prayer without an intention, the objective of the Lawgiver has been met and the obligation has accordingly been fulfilled. However, the muezzin will not receive spiritual reward (*thawāb*) for his call since it was devoid of intention.

Whilst the jurists have differed regarding the prerequisite of intention for the validity of worship, they agree that to act without intention is not spiritually rewarded. This can be seen in the case of minor ablution (*wuḍū'*) and major ablution (*ghusl*). According to the Ḥanafī jurists, intention is not required to make ablution. The majority of scholars disagree, asserting that intention is essential and without it *wuḍū'* or bathing is not achieved. So, this means that if a person were to take a swim in a pond either for leisure or to cool oneself off, then according to the Ḥanafī jurists this person has completed his *wuḍū'* or bath. But according to the majority of jurists *wuḍū'* or *ghusl* is not achieved because intention is an essential requirement without which no act of worship is valid.

The ethical lessons from this maxim are profound. The Qur'an tells us that the sole purpose of human existence on earth is to worship Allah alone without any deistical association with Him. He Most High says, 'I created the jinn and human beings for nothing else but that they may worship Me.' (*al-Dhāriyāt* 51: 56); and 'And worship Allah and join not any partners with Him.' (*al-Nisā'* 4: 36) Human beings are frail, have numerous weaknesses and are prone to temptation. The innate human traits of forgetfulness and ingratitude mean that humans require constant reminders of their covenant to worship Allah. It is because of this weakness and Allah's infinite mercy that He did not forsake His creation. He sent Prophets after Prophets to humankind to remind them and call upon them to worship Him alone. Intrinsic to the meaning of 'worshipping Allah' is that any act of worship must be done solely to please Him alone, and this can only be understood by intention. No other verse in the Qur'an talks more clearly about the importance of sincerity in worshipping Allah than verse five of Surah al-Bayyinah: 'Yet all that they had been commanded was that they worship Allah, with utter sincerity, devoting themselves exclusively to Him, and that they establish prayer and pay Zakāh. This is the Right Faith.'

It is crystal clear that the foundation of worshipping Allah is *not* merely to perform acts of physical and spiritual worship; it is in fact sincerity. No matter how much worship is undertaken and no matter how great the sacrifice is, if these lack sincerity then they amount to nothing. This indeed can be seen in the *ḥadīth qudsī* where the Prophet ﷺ articulates a clear and stark warning of the danger of performing acts of worship with ulterior motives.

> The first of people against whom judgement shall be pronounced on the Day of Resurrection will be a man who has died a martyr. He shall be brought forward and Allah will make known to him His favours and he will recognise them. Allah will say: 'And what did you do about them?' He will say: 'I fought for You until I died a martyr'. Allah will say: 'You have lied! You did but fight that it might be said of you, "he is so courageous."' And so it was said. Then he will be ordered to be dragged along on his face until he is cast into the Hellfire.
>
> Another shall be a man who has studied religious knowledge and has taught it and who used to recite the Qur'an. He shall be brought forward and Allah will make him known to him and His favours and he will recognize them. Allah will say: 'And what did you do about them?' He will say: 'I studied religious knowledge and I taught it

> and recited the Qur'an for Your sake.' Allah will say: 'You have lied! You did but study religious knowledge that it might be said of you: "He is a reciter."' And so it was said. Then he will be ordered to be dragged along on his face until he is cast into the Hellfire.
>
> Another shall be a man whom Allah had made rich and to whom He had given all kinds of wealth. He shall be brought forward and Allah will make him known to him and His favours and he will recognize them. Allah will say: 'And what did you do about them?' He will say: 'I left no path in which You like money to be spent without spending in it for Your sake.' Allah will say: 'You have lied! You did but do so that it might be said of you: "He is generous." And so it was said.' Then he will be ordered to be dragged along on his face until he is cast into the Hellfire. (Muslim, Tirmidhī and Nasā'ī)[11]

Without pure and sincere intention to please Allah, human actions are meaningless, no matter how great the deed or action may be. Abū Umāmah narrates that the Prophet ﷺ said: 'The most beloved thing through which My slave worships Me is sincerity towards Me.' (Aḥmad)

11. Translation taken from Ezzeddin Ibrahim, *Forty Hadith Qudsi*, pp. 52-54 with slight modification.

2

Rewards are According to Intentions

لا ثَوَابَ إلّا بِنِيَّةٍ

There is no reward without intention

This maxim is mostly supported by Ḥanafī jurists. The reason why they promote this maxim lies in their understanding of the relationship between intention and the validity of spiritual worship. The Ḥanafīs maintain that the principle function of intention is for attaining spiritual reward (*thawāb*). The majority of scholars disagree with this. They maintain that intention is not only about attaining spiritual reward. Rather, intention is primarily related to the validity of an act of worship, and the acquisition of spiritual reward is an inevitable consequence automatically gained due to the completion of a good deed. Both groups of scholars equally agree that not every action requires intention for its validity; there are some which require intention for their validity and others which call for no intention.

Acts of worship which entail intention are those which the Lawgiver has made specific acts of worship such as prayer, *zakat*, hajj and the like. Acts of worship which are not specifically demanded by the Lawgiver, but serve as objectives to proper acts of worship are usually the ones that require no intention for their validity. For example, removing filth or impurities from clothes is an act of worship; however, it does not require intention. This is because wearing pure clothes is not an act of worship *per se* but it is only necessary for those acts of worship which demand the wearing of impurity-free clothes. Therefore if garments have come in contact with filth, the objective simply becomes the removal of filth by any way possible. This means that if a person were to walk in the rain and a sufficient amount of rain water falls on the contaminated area and consequently the filth is washed away, the clothes are considered to be rendered pure. This is despite the fact that no intention was made by the person. However, due to the absence of intention no reward can be attained by the person. On the other hand, if a person washes impure clothes with the intention of worship then they will be rewarded accordingly.

In essence, both groups of scholars agree that intention is a condition for the validity of certain acts of worship, the difference between them is what they regard to be the primary function of intention.

If the purpose of life on earth is to act as a place to 'sow the seeds of good deeds to be harvested in the Hereafter' (Bukhārī) then it behoves a Muslim to seek to increase the potential of this metaphorical harvest at every opportunity possible. Making intention of worshipping Allah regardless of how inconsequential the act may seem is a continuous reminder of the purpose of humankind. It has considerable positive implications of God-consciousness—*taqwā*—nourishing the soul, moulding the ego and demanding complete submission to Allah. Intention in all acts of worship reaffirms the cognitive process of worshipping Allah. Moreover, this continuous conscious volition of worshipping Allah elevates a person's status of mediocrity to a level of transcendence—to the station of the great *awliyā'* (friends) of Allah. This should be the aspiration of all true believers.

3

Combining Acts of Worship

الجَمْعُ بَيْنَ عِبادَتَيْنِ بِنِيَّةٍ واحِدَةٍ

Combining two acts of worship with one intention

This maxim explores the possibility of making two intentions for two types of worship simultaneously in one act of worship. This concept is not universally accepted by all scholars, and they differ greatly regarding the details as well as the types of worship permissible to be performed in one act of worship. This theory can be best understood by dividing spiritual worship into two types. First: acts of worship the Lawgiver has demanded their observance, such as prayer, zakat and hajj, termed here as 'proper acts of worship'. Second: the Lawgiver demands certain acts of worship, but these do not constitute proper acts of worship, rather these rituals serve as means to the validity of proper acts of worship termed here as *wasā'il*. If the act of worship is one of the *wasā'il* then the general principle is that it is valid to make two intentions in one act of worship. For example, if on a Friday a person happens to be in the state of major ritual impurity (*janābah*), when bathing, this person intends to remove major ritual impurity as well as bathing for Friday prayers, which is an act of worship as established by the Sunnah. In this case the person successfully achieved both acts of worship, one being a *farḍ* and the other a Sunnah. This is because bathing itself is not a proper act of worship, but a means (*wasā'il*) for the validity of another act of worship. If, however, a person intends to offer two obligatory or voluntary acts of 'proper worship' in a single act of worship, then regard is paid to whether the act of worship is prayer (*ṣalāh*) or another act of worship. If it is prayer, such as combining the Ẓuhr and 'Aṣr prayers in one unit of prayer, then this is improper and invalid. This applies to all types of prayer combination, whether it is compulsory prayers, Sunnah prayers or voluntary. However, Ḥanafī jurists have made an exception and allowed the praying of the *taḥiyyat al-masjid* and the Sunnah of any of the five daily prayers in one unit prayer with one intention.

If it is an act of worship other than prayer then the rule is that the act of worship does not become invalid. Instead the stronger of the two acts of worship in terms of priority and obligation is considered to be executed. For example, a person intends to observe the missed fasts of Ramadan and also the atonement of foreswearing an oath, the fast is considered to be the missed fast of Ramadan. This is because the missed fast of Ramadan has priority and is stronger in terms of obligation than any other types of fasting.

It is noteworthy that it is very difficult to pinpoint precise general rules for cases that contravene the norm. In cases where dual intention is made and a single act of worship is offered, this is subject to a scholarly debate.

Allah commands us in the Qur'an, 'so excel one another in good deeds'. (*al-Baqarah* 2: 148) Seizing every opportunity to make an intention of doing good deeds is certainly a praiseworthy and noble act. Worshipping Allah is based on the fundamental principle of sincerity. Allah, the Lawgiver, has made His law to test humankind, and consequently He has laid down different duties to be performed at different times. If it was permissible to make multiple intentions in a single act of worship, it would inevitably have negative consequences. The concept of 'test' would become defunct by virtue of people praying one prayer a day intending with it all the five daily prayers. Spiritual worship has been spread out at different times of the day and year in order to act as a continuous reminder to humankind about their duty of servitude to Allah. Although Islam encourages copious good deeds, humankind needs to be aware that obedience is about worshipping Allah as He has demanded, on time and when it is due.

4

The Primacy of Intention in Contracts

العِبْرَةُ في العُقُودِ لِلْمَقاصِدِ وَالمَعاني لا لِلْأَلْفاظِ والمَباني

In contracts, regard is paid to intention and meaning rather than to words and forms

This maxim focuses on contractual law. Contracts appear in different forms, reflecting a great variety of situations tailored to addressing the needs of the contracting parties. However, not all jurists agree on this maxim. Although there are circumstances where this maxim is inapplicable, it is by and large accepted by the Ḥanafī, Mālikī and Ḥanbalī jurists. The Shāfiʿī jurists also use this maxim in certain cases, but they generally uphold the contrary maxim: 'In contracts, regard is paid to words and forms rather than to intention and meaning.'[12]

The foundation of contractual law in Shariah is based on the premise that contracts are understood on the basis of the words employed in the contract. This is because words usually reflect the intention of the contracting parties. The word *ma'ānī* literally means 'sense, meaning, import', but in the context of this maxim it denotes the true intention and motive of the contracting parties. However, when there is a conflict between the words and the intent, this maxim states that regard must be paid to intent over any words employed in the transaction. Looking at a couple of examples will help in shedding light on the application of this maxim in Islamic law. It so happens that in the culture of some people the seller sometimes uses playful expressions such as, 'I am giving you this car for free' to engage the prospective buyer in a conversation and begin terms of negotiation. Technically speaking the car becomes a gift to the prospective buyer. But no regard can be paid to any claims of it being a gift because the intent of the seller must be regarded and takes precedence over the actual words used. However,

12. Ibn Nujaym, *al-Ahsbāh*, p. 18; al-Zurqānī, Aḥmad ibn Muḥammad, 1989. *Sharḥ al-Qawā'id al-Fiqhiyyah*, Damascus: Dār al-Qalam, p. 55; Ismā'īl, Muḥammad Bakr, 1997. *Al-Qawā'id al-Fiqhiyyah Bayn al-Aṣālah wa al-Tawjīh*, Cairo: Dār al-Manār, p. 39; Diyah, 'Abd al-Majīd 'Abdullāh, 2005. *Al-Qawā'id wa al-Ḍawābiṭ al-Fiqhiyyah li-Aḥkām al-Mabī' fī al-Sharī'ah al-Islāmiyyah*, Jordon; Dār al-Nafā'is, p. 332.

where a person wanting to buy a can of drink asks the shopkeeper its price and receives the reply, 'don't worry about it' can be considered to mean that the shopkeeper has gifted the can to the person. Two things support this interpretation: firstly custom and secondly it is most likely that the intention of the shopkeeper means he does not want to charge for the can of drink.

Likewise, if a person was to buy something but tells the seller, 'take my watch as *amānah* (a trust)' then the object left with the seller is collateral (*rahn*) and not *amānah* and the rules of *rahn* will apply. This means that any objects left as *amānah* with the seller cannot be sold off and remains the property of the buyer. The rules of *rahn*, on the other hand, imply that if the buyer fails to pay for the merchandise the seller has the right to sell the *rahn* to recover the cost of his merchandise.

Human life reflects interdependence on other humans. It is not possible to envisage human life without commerce and trading. One of the primary objectives of the Shariah is to eliminate disputes and fighting. Buying and selling is an institution woven into the fabric of human societies. The most frequently occurring contractual matter is trading. Barely a day passes in most people's life where they have not engaged in buying and selling in one form or another. Due to the frequency of this,

Islam has laid down strict rules governing transactions. In Shariah the main objective of transactions is to facilitate the smooth transfer of properties from one person to another. It is for this reason that Shariah does not pay regard to only words or intentions but considers both in understanding the true object of the transaction. It is a moral obligation to consider the property of others as inviolable and sacrosanct. This is an unequivocal moral obligation which Allah commands us to observe: 'O you who believe, do not usurp one another's properties wrongfully; rather, let there be trading by mutual consent.' (*al-Nisā'* 4: 29)

5

Intent Takes Precedence over Words

العِبْرَةُ بِالإِرَادَةِ لا بِاللَّفْظِ

Greater consideration is paid to intent
and not to words

Ibn Qayyim al-Jawziyyah mentions this maxim in his book *I'lām al-Muwaqqi'īn*.[13] The general rule of *uṣūl al-fiqh* is that the specific (*khāṣṣ*) remains specific and cannot be construed to have a general connotation; while a general (*'āmm*) expression can be reduced to having a specific element. This maxim goes against this principle in the sense that a word can be employed with a specific connotation yet it can be understood in its general sense provided this

13. Ibn al-Qayyim, *I'lām al-Muwaqqi'īn*, vol. 1, p. 219; Ismā'īl, Muḥammad Bakr, 1997. *Al-Qawā'id al-Fiqhiyyah Bayn al-Aṣālah wa al-Tawjīh*, Cairo: Dār al-Manār, p. 35.

was the intention of the speaker. For example, if a person was invited to dinner but says, 'by Allah I do not take dinner', or 'go to sleep', where he replies, 'by Allah I won't sleep' or 'drink this water' and he responds, 'by Allah I won't drink'. Although all these words have been expressed in a general sense yet its meaning is construed to imply a specific meaning. This can only be assumed to be the case due to the intention of the speaker. Intention having a greater weight than the actual spoken words can be seen in a case where a person is coerced to pronounce blasphemous words that according to the Islamic teachings would take a person out of the fold of Islam. Yet Muslim scholars are unanimous in declaring that no act of blasphemy has taken place, arguing that the intention of the speaker must be taken into consideration. Allah says in the Qur'an, 'Whoever disbelieves in Allah after his belief ... except for one who is coerced [to renounce his religion] while his heart is secure in faith. But those who [willingly] open their breasts to disbelief, upon them is the wrath of Allah, and for them is a great punishment.' (*al-Naḥl* 16: 106)

This maxim, if taken on its absolute term, has a very broad implication. However, it was never assigned to be taken in its absolute sense. In Shariah regard is paid to both intention and words, the context of precedence of intent over words or vice versa is worked out by the context and the nature of the contract. An anecdote to support this maxim is mentioned in the *Muṣannaf* of Wakīʿ, which states that, a case was brought to the attention of ʿUmar ibn al-Khaṭṭāb where a woman asked her husband to give her a nickname. The husband complied calling her al-Ṭaybah. The wife was not happy with this asking him to call her something else. The man asked her what she would like him to call her. She replied call me, '*khaliyyah ṭāliq*' (unloved divorced). Thereupon the man said to her, 'you are *khaliyyah ṭāliq*' (unloved divorced). The woman then claimed that her husband had divorced her. ʿUmar did not grant this woman a divorce because she tricked her husband into saying words he did not intend or mean.[14] Hence, at times certain cases must be judged according to their own merits taking into consideration the context and weighing up whether intention or words have a greater significance.

Allah warns Muslims to be aware of the words they utter, 'he [man] does not utter any word except that with him is an observer at hand [recording everything].' (*Qāf* 50: 16) Every word is accounted and every word has meaning, implications and consequences. Although in juristic thought, intention plays a crucial role in determining legal consequences, in spirituality less attention is paid to the intention and more focus is paid to the oral expression. It is for this reason that the Prophet ﷺ

14. Ibid.

urged anyone who believes in Allah and the Last Day to say good things or remain silent (Bukhārī and Muslim). In another hadith the Prophet ﷺ described an ideal Muslim to be the one from whom others are safe from his tongue and hands (Bukhārī). This means one should be careful of any hurt that may be caused due to inappropriate words regardless of how well intended the statement was meant to be.

6

The Explicit Has Primacy over the Implicit

لا عِبْرَةَ لِلدَّلالَةِ في مُقابَلَةِ التَّصْريحِ

No consideration is paid to implication when explication is found[15]

Evidence is the fundamental apparatus in a legal system. If any claim is made then it must be substantiated with proof. It is reported that the Prophet ﷺ said: 'If people were given on the basis of their claims, some men would claim the wealth and lives of other people. Rather proof is required from whoever makes a claim and an oath from whomever denies it.' (al-Bayhaqī) Evidence can be either circumstantial or conclusive. If it is circumstantial then

15. Ismā'īl, Muḥammad Bakr, 1997. *Al-Qawā'id al-Fiqhiyyah Bayn al-Aṣālah wa al-Tawjīh*, Cairo: Dār al-Manār, p. 50.

it is referred to as *dalīl ẓannī*, and *dalīl qaṭ'ī* if it is conclusive. This maxim stipulates that no consideration can be paid to inferred evidence suggesting the obligation of doing something or otherwise, or the lawfulness or unlawfulness of something when there is explicit proof suggesting otherwise. Explicit evidence must take precedence and all other proof must be disregarded.

When understanding evidence it is important to take into consideration context, which will play a crucial role in grading the quality of the evidence into either *dalīl ẓannī* or *dalīl qaṭ'ī*. The following examples will help elucidate this maxim. Allah has mentioned in the Qur'an a list of persons' homes which do not require prior permission for a person to enter and help themselves to food.[16] If a person were to enter such a house and start to eat from a plate of food he finds, and during this process the plate accidentally falls from his hands and breaks, in this case, that person will not be legally obliged to pay for the damage or replace it. Although the verse only mentions eating freely at those houses and says nothing about breaking cutlery or tableware, the

16. Allah says, 'There is no blame on the blind nor any blame on the sick nor on yourselves that you eat in your own houses, or your fathers' houses, or your brothers' houses, or your sisters', or your paternal uncles', or your paternal aunties', or your maternal uncles', or your maternal aunties', or in the houses whose keys you possess, or the house of your friends. There is no blame whether you eat together or separately.' (*al-Nūr* 24: 61)

inferred rule is since that person has been allowed to enter and eat from the house, it suggests that any accidental damage caused to the utensils or cutlery has no consequence, much as if the owner himself were to break the plate. This is contrary to when the owner explicitly prohibits that person from entering his house and despite this the person enters and breaks the plate. In this case the person is now legally obliged to replace or pay for the damage. The reason why he is responsible is because we have explicit evidence prohibiting him from entering the house which overrides the inferred evidence, and therefore responsibility is now established; much like if he were to enter the house of any other person and damage any property therein.

We are morally obliged to look for clarity and be certain of any course of action we may take. *Ẓann* or speculative thinking can have an insidious effect on human psychology and in extreme cases it can cause paranoia. Allah commands Muslims to ascertain the quality of the information one receives, 'O you who believe, if there comes to you a disobedient one with information, investigate it, lest you harm a people out of ignorance and become, over what you have done, regretful.' (*al-Ḥujurāt* 49: 6) Therefore, if there is implicit evidence in contrast to explicit instructions, preference must be given to the explicit over the implicit.

7

When to Give Preference to Others

الإيثارُ بالقُرَبِ مَكْروهٌ وفي غَيْرِها مَحْبُوبٌ

Giving preference to others over oneself in acts of worship is disliked but laudable in all other circumstances[17]

This maxim deals with setting the priority for Muslims with respect to worshipping Allah. Not only does this maxim have a legal corollary but a spiritual one too. In fact, the spiritual significance seems to almost render the legal implication a subtle hint. The attitude of every good believer is that he should strive to earn as much spiritual reward (*thawāb*) as possible. It is inarguable that life on earth is finite and uncertain. For some, their lifespan

17. Ismā'īl, Muḥammad Bakr, 1997. *Al-Qawā'id al-Fiqhiyyah Bayn al-Aṣālah wa al-Tawjīh*, Cairo: Dār al-Manār, p. 50.

is a few weeks, for others a few decades, and for others many decades. If the appointed time of death is unknown and the purpose of life on earth is to 'sow the seeds of good deeds to be harvested in the Hereafter' (Bukhārī), then this demands a certain level of selfish behaviour in acquiring this valuable spiritual reward. That is to say it is only logical that human life on earth is of a limited period, not knowing if today is going to be the last day on earth, hence one should seize every opportunity to pursue doing good deeds, taking his own interest over others. For example, if a person has enough water to make ablution for himself only, he should use that water to make ablution and not give the water to this fellow brother to make ablution only to be forced to make *tayammum* (substitute ablution) himself. This is because ablution with water is far superior to making *tayammum* and therefore it is far more virtuous. It seems to be self-defeating to give another person the opportunity to gain spiritual reward whilst depriving oneself of it. Likewise, if a person is better qualified in terms of knowledge and a melodious voice and the appointed mosque imam is absent, he should seize the opportunity to lead the prayer or call the *adhān* rather than offering others to do it. A common practice in some communities is to offer the first row to the senior aged out of respect and courtesy. This maxim stipulates that the first comers should occupy the first row and this opportunity should be not passed to others. It is narrated that the Prophet ﷺ said, 'If people knew the virtue of calling the *adhān* and standing in the first row in prayer, and if they had no other choice, but drawing lots [in order that they could be the one to call for prayer and stand in the first line], they would go for drawing lots ...' (Bukhārī)

The Qur'an encourages us to compete in doing as many good deeds as possible, 'so let all aspirants aspire after that.' (*al-Muṭaffifīn* 83: 26) It warns us of the day that no soul can afford assistance to another, 'And fear the Day when no soul will suffice for another soul, nor will intercession be accepted from it, nor will compensation be taken from it, nor will they be aided.' (*al-Baqarah* 2: 48) Therefore it must be the duty of all Muslims to seize every opportunity to capitalise on doing good deeds. This is the desired behaviour regarding religious matters, but regarding non-religious issues Islam encourages a person to be thoughtful, generous and kind, and give preference to others first and secondly to oneself. Allah tells us in the Qur'an, 'They love those who emigrated to them and find not any want in their breast of what they [i.e. the emigrants] were given but give them preference over themselves, even though they are in privation. And whoever is protected from the stinginess of his soul—it is those who will be successful.' (*al-Ḥashr* 59: 9)

8

Intention in Devotional and Other Acts

المَقاصِدُ والاعْتِقاداتُ مُعْتَبَرَةٌ في التَّصَرُّفاتِ والعِباراتِ
كما هي مُعْتَبَرَةٌ في القُرُباتِ والعِباداتِ

Regard is paid to intention and belief in transactions, and expressions as they are in acts of good deeds and worship[18]

Ibn al-Qayyim al-Jawziyyah asserts that intention has the power to render something to be considered lawful or unlawful, valid or invalid, obedience or disobedience. Here are few examples to illustrate how this maxim is applied. For example, if a person were to slaughter an animal with the intention of eating it, that would be lawful for him. However, if he were to intend the animal as a sacrifice for

18. Ibn al-Qayyim, *I'lām al-Muwaqqi'īn*, vol. 3, pp. 95-96.

any other deity, the animal becomes unlawful for Muslim consumption. In a case where a person not in state of *iḥrām* were to hunt for a person in a state of *iḥrām* (*muḥrim*), it would be unlawful for them to eat the game. But if the person were to hunt it for a non-*muḥrim* then it would be lawful for a *muḥrim* to eat from it. Likewise, if a person were to press grapes with the intention of making wine, it would be sinful, but if it were pressed for any other purpose there is no harm. Another very good example of how regard is paid to intention and conviction can be seen in a case of *ẓihār*. *Ẓihār* is a pre-Islamic form of divorce outlawed by Islam due to its cruel nature. It is invoked by a man describing his wife to be to him like the 'back of his mother'. By saying this, the woman was neither divorced nor married to the man, thus depriving her of moving on in her life, although the man was at liberty to do so. However, if a man were to say to his wife 'you are unto me like my mother' with the intention of meaning anything other than *ẓihār*, no consequences apply. In each of these cases the Islamic legal ruling could have gone either way, but it was intention that determined it.

Getting intentions and convictions correct should be the utmost priority for all Muslims. True intentions can only be known by Allah and the person making the intention. As previously discussed (see: Maxim 1) on the Day of Judgement we will be held to account first and foremost for our intentions. Our intentions must reflect the intention to do good, be just and avoid causing any harm. Allah has made it a moral stipulation for men wishing to take back their wives after a revocable divorce that they have intention and conviction to do good to their wives, 'and their husbands have more right to take them back [in this period] if they want reconciliation.' (*al-Baqarah* 2: 228), The moral obligation of intending to do good deeds by way of fairness can also be seen in the case of inheritance. That is to say, if a person attempts to be unfair in his division of the estate, Allah has given the heirs the right to rectify this by either ratifying the decision of the deceased or changing the division of the estate to be concordant with the Qur'anic law of inheritance. (*al-Baqarah* 2: 182)

9

The Principle of Removing Harm

الضَّرَرُ يُزَالُ

Harm is to be removed

This is the second core maxim. The grandeur of its legal significance has led some to argue that this maxim encompasses half of the Shariah.[19] This is because one of the prime objectives of Islamic law is to remove harm (*mafsadah*) and secure benefit (*maṣlaḥah*). This implies that all of Allah's law is aimed at bringing about benefit and preventing harm. Upon this understanding, al-Būṭī has defined harm (*ḍarar*) as anything that impedes the achievement

19. Al-Nadwī, 'Ali Aḥmad, 1991. *Al-Qawā'id al-Fiqhiyyah: Mafhūmu-hā, Nash'atu-hā, Taṭawwuru-hā, Darāsat Mu'allafā-ti-hā, Adillatiu-hā, Mahammatu-hā, Taṭbīqāti-hā,* Damascus: Dār al-Qalam, p. 252.

of benefit (*maṣlaḥah*) as a result of infringement, arbitrariness or negligence.[20] The authority of this maxim is derived from numerous Qur'anic verses and Prophetic traditions. The prohibition of causing harm is mentioned more than ten times in the Qur'an, but the more direct precept can be found in the Prophetic tradition recorded by Mālik and others: 'There is no causing harm or reciprocating harm.' This means that it is unlawful for a person to do or say anything to cause unlawful harm to anyone, and likewise if anyone has been harmed, it is unlawful for that person to reciprocate in causing harm. The word *ḍarar* employed in the Prophetic tradition and adopted in the maxim is used in a general context and therefore encompasses all types of harm, whether it be physical, verbal, psychological; regardless of whether it has occurred or is imminent.

There are three conditions that must be observed in order to ascertain harm:

1. The harm must be real and certain (*mutaḥaqqaq*). This means that harm must presently exist or it is most likely to exist in the near future. Therefore, if harm is only a perceived factor and uncertain (*mutawahham*) then this maxim cannot apply.
2. The harm must be excessive (*fāḥish*). If the harm is slight and negligible then no consideration is paid to that. The measurement of

20. Al-Būṭī, Muḥammad Sa'īd Ramaḍān, 1982. *Ḍawābiṭ al-Maṣlahah fī al-Sharī'ah al-Islāmiyyah*, Damascus: Dār al-Fikr, p. 40.

'excessive' is subjective and usually determined by the merits of the case, or if it is widespread it is determined by custom (*'urf*).

3. The harm must be unlawful or unjustified. However, if the harm is lawful, such as demanding a thief to be punished, then although the punishment is reciprocating harm it is nevertheless lawful and therefore not considered as 'reciprocating harm' as mentioned in the hadith.

Here is an example to explain the application of this maxim. If a person were to build a tall building overshadowing the property of his neighbour, thus blocking the sun's rays which causes the neighbour harm in terms of harming plants, feeling the sun's rays thus being deprived of its heat and light, this is a cause of harm. The harm is real, excessive and unlawful. This is contrary to a case where the person erects a temporary construction for a few days, because none of the above conditions are found.

Such is the ethical code of Islam that does not tolerate unreasonable behaviour in terms of causing harm or reciprocating harm. It must be the natural approach of every Muslim to do his utmost not to cause any harm whatsoever to anyone else regardless of race or religion. It is related the Prophet Muḥammad ﷺ ordered anyone who consumed raw garlic and onions not to attend the mosques (Muslim) simply because the odious breath caused by garlic and onions will cause offence and harm to fellow worshippers. If not even this slight act of offence was left unadmonished, then how can acts greater than this be tolerated in Islam? Islam's ethical code of conduct demands peaceful co-existence, if it cannot be achieved amicably then the authorities must enforce it by any means possible. Abū Dāwūd records in his *Sunan* that a *ṣaḥābī* owned a single date palm in an orchard belonging to another *ṣaḥābī*. The owner of the tree frequently visited his tree, and this eventually started to cause the orchard owner, who lived there with his family, inconvenience due to a lack of privacy. The orchard owner requested the owner of the tree to sell it to him, but he refused. He then requested him to transplant it to another location, but he refused. The orchard owner then went to the Prophet ﷺ and requested him to convince the tree owner. The Prophet ﷺ attempted to do so but the man refused, not even the certain reward of the Hereafter could persuade the man to give up his claim to the tree. At that point the Prophet ﷺ told him, 'you are causing harm' and then instructed the orchard owner to simply uproot the date palm.

10

Balancing Competing Harms

يُحْتَمَلُ الضَّرَرُ الخاصُّ لِدَفْعِ ضَرَرٍ عامٍّ

Private harm is endured in order to suppress public harm

The application of this maxim can be best illustrated in a case where there are two problems at hand and doing either one of them will cause harm. But one of the issues affects only a few people while the other affects many. In such a situation priority is given to suppressing the harm a large number of people will experience over the harm a few people will have to endure. A few examples will help elucidate this maxim. A person living by the road has a wall which has suffered structural damage. There is a reasonable possibility that the wall will collapse, potentially hurting pedestrians or other road users.

This potential harm is weighed against the financial harm that proprietor will have to bear. The outcome is that the owner has to pay for the demolition or repair cost for the wall. Compulsory purchase orders are another good example to show the use of this maxim. A person owns real estate or even a house which has come to obstruct planning for roads. The roads are vital to transportation for the masses. Circumventing that land will generate more problems, hence leaving no option but to build road through that plot of land. The case where the owner refuses to sell the land creates two types of independent harm. On one hand, harm will be caused to the owner, who may have been living on that land for many generations and moving will cause him emotional upset as well as probable inconvenience, such as access to local amenities. On the other hand, the lack of thoroughfare is causing many hundreds of people harm on a daily basis. Weighing up both harms it becomes apparent that only a few people will be harmed in one case, namely the owner and his family; while on the other hand, the general public faces great hardship without the road. In such a case the owner will be offered compensation for his land and if he refuses the courts can force him to leave.

The aim in Islam is to eliminate all types of harm to anybody. However, human life is not as simple as that and at times certain situations arise where causing harm becomes inevitable. Where harm becomes unavoidable, the ethical and moral course in Islam is to limit it to the least harmful act. Although these cases involve causing harm, it nevertheless falls into the ambit of the Qur'anic ethico-legal precept of cooperating on good and piety which Allah has enjoined in the Qur'an. He says: 'And cooperate in righteousness and piety, but do not cooperate in sin and aggression. And fear Allah; indeed, Allah is severe in penalty'. (*al-Mā'idah* 5: 2) This verse is also the authority of this maxim.

11

The Removal of Harm Takes Precedence

دَرْءُ المَفاسِدِ أَوْلَى مِنْ جَلْبِ المَصالِحِ

Averting Evil is Preferable to Securing Benefit

This is a maxim of the utmost importance and has a versatile application in Muslim law. Its simplicity is overshadowed by the subtlety of its implication and application. The authority for this maxim can be found in the Qur'an and the teachings of the Prophet Muḥammad ﷺ. For example, Allah says in the Qur'an: 'They ask you about wine and gambling. Say: "There is great sin in both and some benefit for people. But the sin is greater than the benefit." (*al-Baqarah* 2: 219) This verse highlights two things: firstly there are some benefits in wine and gambling, and secondly there is harm in wine and gambling. The obvious benefits of wine are its taste, its intoxicating buzz, commercial and financial gain and the like.

Other benefits may not be so obvious, for example recent medical research shows that consuming a moderate amount of wine has benefits because it contains antioxidants and resveratrol which are good for the heart and circulatory system. The same can be said about the benefits of gambling where a substantial amount can be earned in a very short period with very little effort. Yet despite the apparent superficial benefits of alcohol and gambling, their harmfulness needs no elaboration. Hence, in making the choice between the harm and the benefit of alcohol and gambling precedence is given to averting the harm, and the minor benefit is disregarded. In a similar manner, the Prophet Muḥammad ﷺ opted to avert creating sedition by disregarding the benefit that would have been brought by restructuring the Ka'bah upon the original foundations.[21] When he was asked by 'Ā'ishah, 'why don't you return it back to its original foundation', the Prophet ﷺ replied, 'had it not been for the fact that your people were recently immersed in disbelief I would have done it'. (Bukhārī and Muslim) The reason for the Prophet's decision was because the Ka'bah was always honoured and sanctified by the Arabs, and intentionally demolishing it to rebuild it would have caused uproar, due to the recent conversion to Islam. The Prophet ﷺ knew that the people could not

21. The original shape of the Ka'bah was rectangular, but a flood damaged the Ka'bah beyond repair. During the rebuilding of the Ka'bah, the Makkans fell short of finance and so decided that they would keep it in a cuboid shape.

understand the reason behind his action, and therefore it would create confusion, upset and vexation. So the Prophet ﷺ decided to leave it, because averting harm takes priority over the benefit it would bring.

Its application in Muslim law has profound consequences and is applied in many aspects and issues of law. For example, the sale of alcohol, pork, lottery tickets and the like has many commercial and economic benefits but the harm of religiously proscribed products being available in the markets takes priority over the commercial gain that would be made. The application of this in the political field can be seen in a case of rebellion against an unjust ruler. There are many hadiths which have prohibited this action.[22] The process of removing an unjust ruler will lead to the loss of many lives and the destruction of properties and infrastructure. But there is no guarantee that the successor will be just or any different than the tyrant he is replacing. The harm that will come about due to rebellion is greater than the benefits it will bring.[23] However, if the rebellion is certain to succeed with the minimum of destruction and a certainty that the replacement will be far better than the present then that is a different matter altogether.

22. See: Bukhārī, Hadith No. 6647; Muslim, Hadith Nos. 4877, 4882, 4888, 4891, 4892.
23. See: Al-Nawawī, Muḥyī al-Dīn, 1996. *Al-Minhāj Sharḥ Ṣaḥīḥ Muslim*, Beirut; Dār al-Maʿrifah, edited by Khalīl Ma'mūn Shīḥā, third edition, 12: 224.

In Islam the principle is always to suppress harm. Therefore, if a case arises where there is a need to choose between harm and benefit, then preventing harm has priority over the benefit that may be gained. The reason why averting harm has more priority than bringing about benefit rests on the logic that if harm or evil is eradicated then that will automatically bring about goodness. But if benefit coexists with harm or evil and bringing about benefit is given preference over eradicating harm, then in actual fact evil will grow and fester in society. The benefit will only temporarily mask harm. On the other hand, if harm is repelled then benefit will subsequently be allowed to manifest and flourish. It is a moral obligation that every member of society works toward eradicating harm. This maxim seeks to encourage the removal of selfish individualism and exhorts people to look beyond personal gain for the betterment of everyone.

12

When the Unlawful Becomes Permitted

الضَّرُوراتُ تُبيحُ المَحْظوراتِ

Dire exigency renders lawful the unlawful

This is a fascinating maxim and so pertinent to human life. This maxim provides a sense of magnanimous dispensation in Islam, and grants leeway at a time when a person has his back to the wall with no way out. Instead of breaking the law, the otherwise unlawful now becomes lawful for a person in dire exigency. Identifying dire exigency is subjective and it is judged on a case by case basis. What may be dire exigency for one person may not be for another, therefore there are some guidelines to be observed in order to avoid people using this maxim to meet their vain desires:

1. The dire exigency is considered to be real only in a situation of life and death or the loss of property.
2. The exigency must be present and not something predicted.
3. There is no other lawful alternative.
4. If it is a special case, such as a person needing to take medicine which contains alcohol or any other unlawful ingredients, then a specialist in that field must be consulted.

The authority of this maxim can be found in many Qur'anic verses. For instance, Allah instructs the believers, 'Indeed [Allah] has forbidden for you carrion, blood, pork and any animals [slaughtered] with other than Allah's name. But if anyone is forced [to eat such things] by necessity, rather than transgression or excess, he commits no sin.' (*al-Baqarah* 2: 173) In another verse Allah tells the believers, 'Unlawful for you to eat is carrion, blood, pork and any animals [slaughtered] with other than Allah's name ... But if anyone is forced by hunger with no intention of doing wrong, Allah is Most Forgiving, Most Merciful.' (*al-Mā'idah* 5: 3) These two verses clearly and categorically exonerate a Muslim of any blame for consuming unlawful foodstuff when they are in a situation of dire exigency. This concept can be extended to cover any situation where a person is forced to do something unlawful to preserve his life and property. The application of this maxim can be seen in various cases in Islamic law.

For instance, if a person is threatened with his life to utter blasphemous words, which would normally take him out of the fold of Islam, then uttering those words has no consequence on his faith. If a person is stranded and has no alternative liquid to drink except wine and fears death due to thirst then drinking wine becomes lawful for him to the extent that prevents death. In a case where a person has an operation and needs a blood transfusion or otherwise will die, it becomes lawful for him to receive the blood transfusion although blood is considered impure in Islam.

For every true believer the commandments of Allah are a serious matter. The moral and ethical code in Islam demands Muslims to respect the boundaries (*himā*) of Allah, contemplating not to even to approach it let alone transgress it. In any cases where a true believer is forced to break the law of Allah, he will experience in his conscience a moral dilemma: how can he transgress the laws of Allah? This maxim reassures the believer that no sin, no fault and no blame are levied against him. This maxim is a perfect example of Allah's mercy towards His creation; no obligation of providing dispensation is binding upon Allah. If He wanted He could have kept the rule as it was. Yet it was His love for His creation, knowing only too well of their weaknesses, that Allah has granted a dispensation to humankind to violate His law and regard the unlawful as lawful in cases of dire necessity. Allah Himself declares in the Qur'an that no sin, no moral impediment can be levelled against a person trapped in dire exigency.

13

Proportionality in Exigent Circumstances

ما أُبيحَ للضَّرورَةِ يقَدَّرُ بقَدْرِها

Whatever is rendered lawful due to dire exigency must be proportionate to the need

This maxim is a constraint (*ḍābiṭ*) to its corollary maxim, 'dire exigency renders the unlawful lawful.' This maxim makes clear how and to what extent the corollary maxim can be applied. The reason for this is because dire exigency has made something normally regarded as unlawful (haram) to lawful (halal) for the purpose of preserving life and wealth. Because it is a matter of exceptional urgency the unlawful object which becomes lawful on a temporary basis was to prevent death, loss of limb or destruction of property, it therefore follows that this temporary lawfulness only extends to the point of fulfilling that particular need and nothing more.

For instance, if a person fears that he will die should he not consume haram meat and no other alternative is available, then he must eat only that amount which addresses the 'need', to wit, save himself from hunger; anymore would be unlawful. Another example of its application is disclosing the private area of the body (*'awrah*) to medical professionals. Although the strict rules of modesty stipulate that the *'awrah* must be covered at all times, yet it is permissible to disclose the *'awrah* for medical examinations. However, only that part of the *'awrah* can be disclosed which needs to be examined and nothing more. The authority of this maxim can be found in many Qur'anic verses. For instance, Allah instructs the believers: 'Indeed [Allah] has forbidden for you carrion, blood, pork and any animals [slaughtered] with other than Allah's name. But if anyone is forced [to eat such things] by necessity, **rather than transgression or excess**, he commits no sin.' (*al-Baqarah* 2: 173) In another verse Allah tells the believers, 'Unlawful for you to eat is carrion, blood, pork and any animals [slaughtered] with other than Allah's name ... **But if anyone is forced by hunger with no intention of doing wrong,** Allah is Most Forgiving, Most Merciful.' (*al-Mā'idah* 5: 3) Allah ordains in these verses that 'transgression, excess or wrong doing' must be avoided. These verses explain that no permission to do the unlawful exists when the dire necessity ends.

Taqwā is the moral message of this maxim. The haram remains haram, but only in cases of dire exigency is it temporarily suspended. The amount, extent or volume of the unlawful which has become lawful depends on individual circumstances. A smaller person will need less to drink to meet the needs of his thirst, while a bigger person will require more. But who can tell? Perhaps a person forced by circumstance to drink wine finds that he quite enjoys the taste of wine, so he decides to take advantage of it and consumes more than what is necessary. This is obviously sinful, but this maxim highlights the moral and ethical code of conduct demanded of believers, that is to say, to show self-restraint and fear of Allah, Who knows every action and thought in the minds of men. This legal maxim beautifully reflects the ethico-spiritual message captured in this verse: 'You can warn only him who follows the admonition and fears the Merciful Lord without seeing Him. Give such a person glad tidings of forgiveness and a generous reward. We shall raise the dead to life and We record what they did and the traces of their deeds that they have left behind. We have encompassed that in a Clear Book. (*Yā Sīn* 36: 11-12)

14

Degrees of Exigency

الحاجَةُ تُنَزَّلُ مَنْزِلَةَ الضَّرورَةِ

Dire need is treated the same as dire exigency

This maxim is a corollary of maxim 12: 'Dire exigency renders lawful the unlawful'. Although 'need' (*ḥājah*) becomes the same as 'dire exigency' (*ḍarūrah*) yet its application is distinct. In the case of dire exigency the unlawful becomes lawful. This transformation of legal ruling (*ḥukm sharʿī*) occurs only due to life and death situations. 'Need' on the other hand, is understood as aspects of life so intrinsic to human life that without it life becomes extremely difficult. This means, matters considered questionable in nature but not categorically unlawful (because its unlawfulness has not been established by conclusive evidence from the Qur'an) now becomes permissible in order to address the dire need. So in cases of dire need alcohol, pork and the like will not become lawful, those proscribed items only become lawful in situations of dire exigency.

A few examples will help make it clearer. In many countries cars have become a vital necessity. The problem is the dilemma that in many countries the state legislation demands that drivers must take out insurance in order to drive a car. Insurance policies are problematic contracts deemed to be unlawful according to Islamic law. Therefore, if the circumstances are such that a person needs a car and without it his daily life becomes extremely difficult then taking out insurance is permissible for him. Likewise, some scholars are of the view that taking photos is prohibited due to the hadith recorded by Bukhārī, Muslim and others. However, they deem it as permissible for the purposes of obtaining passports or other official documentation on the grounds of dire need.

The authority for this maxim is extrapolated from the famous Prophetic tradition permitting *salam* transaction. (Bukhārī) Whereas the principle of commercial transactions is that exchange of commodities must exist and must take place at the time of the contract—in a *salam* transaction the money is paid up front but the delivery of the merchandise is agreed at a later date. This was permitted by the Prophet ﷺ due to 'dire need'. That is to say, because it was an established cultural practice of the Madinan Muslims, predicated on providing financial stability while at the same time eliminating deception (*gharar*), meant that *salam* contracts were lawful.

This was allowed in order to meet the 'dire need' of people, and hence a questionable transaction was allowed.

There is a great moral and ethical lesson to be learnt from this maxim. Allah explains His principle of demanding worship from His creation: 'Allah does not burden a soul more than what it can bear'. (*al-Baqarah* 2: 286) In another verse Allah says: 'Allah wants ease and not hardship for you.' (*al-Baqarah* 2: 185) The gentle nature of the Shariah aims to inculcate the optimal behavioural conduct a person ought to have with other humans. Those in senior positions able to impose their authority should proceed with caution, ensuring that what they demand their subordinate to do is within their ability. Any instruction should be given being mindful of whether the person instructed is capable of doing it, taking into consideration the person's physical, psychological and intellectual capacity. This maxim aims to teach humankind the magnanimity of Allah. If Allah's approach is to make life easy then humans are more worthy of emulating this approach.

15

Considerations in the Removal of Harm

الضَّرَرُ لا يُزالُ بالضَّرَرِ

Harm is not replaced by harm

The condition for the application of this maxim is that harm cannot be replaced with harm that is greater than the present harm. It seems self-defeating to remove harm if it is only replaced by a similar harm, or worse. Rather, the aim in Islam is to eliminate harm completely, if not, then as much as possible. The legal import of this maxim is found more in personal and commercial law, with little significance in spiritual law. The maxim has various applications in Shariah. For example, a house is owned jointly by more than one person and one of the co-owners wants to divide the house and partition his area off in order to get his own privacy. However, the problem is that the house is too small to be divided. In fact, the division of the house would not only cause everyone harm but would make selling the house in future very difficult indeed. In this case it can be seen that one of the owners is facing harm due to the lack of privacy, but his suggestion to divide the house into parts causes greater harm than what he is enduring. The solution can only be that one of the other co-owners should buy him out or another buyer is found. Another example of the application of this maxim is where a person would like to extend his house to provide more space for his family. However, if his proposed plans for extension would cause his neighbours great harm then no permission for extension can be granted, and if the extension is made prior to the neighbour's consent then a request to demolish it can be made or compensation is rendered to the neighbour.

It is related in the authentic books of hadith that the Prophet ﷺ was once sitting with his Companions and he told them, 'He will not enter Paradise from whose harm his neighbour is not safe.' (Muslim) The concept of harming and causing harm revolves around eliminating harm. What Islam aims at achieving is trying to find a solution to the problem and not to compound it. Therefore, the ethical code in Islam is to seek a solution through patience and fear of God. Replacing a problem with a greater or similar problem solves nothing, and rather than a few people enduring hardship many people will become affected, causing infringements to their rights and liberties. Allah exhorts the believers to be fearful of Allah and exercise patience and then success will be achieved: 'O believers, be steadfast, and vie in steadfastness, stand firm in your faith, and hold Allah in fear that you may attain true success.' (*Āl 'Imrān* 3: 200)

16

Taking the Lesser of Two Evils

إذا تعارَضَتْ مَفْسَدَتان رُوْعِيَ أعْظَمُهُما ضَرَرًا
بارْتِكابِ أخَفِّهِما

When two evils are present, the greater evil is
disregarded in favour of the lesser evil

This maxim resonates the fact that human life is not always a simple colour of black and white, where choices are simple and presented in simple forms. Indeed it is a part of human life that in certain circumstances people are faced with two choices, neither of which will be without grave consequences. Regardless, one thing is certain; a decision has to be made. In such a case the lesser of the two evils is performed. This is applicable when only two options are available and no viable third alternative is available. A few examples will help illustrate how this maxim is applied. In a case of an abnormal pregnancy, where the foetus has developed in such a way that it threatens the life of the mother, leaving the only option of either the unborn child surviving or the mother. Whatever course of action is taken one thing is certain; there will be grave consequences, to wit, the loss of life. That is to say, if the unborn child is allowed to live then it will cause the mother to die, and if the mother is to be saved then the unborn child has to be terminated. In such a situation, weighing up the two cases, it seems that the evil of aborting the unborn child is a lesser evil than allowing the mother to die. This is because the mother's life is established; she has a role, duty, career, responsibility to others and much more, which is real and functional, whereas the life of the unborn child has none of these. Furthermore, the life of the unborn child is not certain while the life of the mother is certain. Another example can be seen in a case of conjoined twins who require an operation to separate them. If this operation is not done then it is most likely that both of them will die, but if the operation is done, there is a chance that both of them can survive, although this is highly risky. In this situation, a case to go ahead with the operation to separate the two twins can be made.

The authority of this maxim has been extrapolated from the famous hadith about a Bedouin who entered the Prophet's mosque in Madinah and urinated against the wall. Some of the Companions stood up to approach the man but the Prophet ﷺ

stopped them and told them to let the Bedouin finish. After he had finished the Prophet ﷺ instructed his Companions to pour a bucket of water over the urine (Muslim). Here the Prophet ﷺ weighed the consequences of removing that man forcefully or letting him finish. The consequence of disrupting him while he was in full flow would cause the man harm. Moreover, the urine would defile a wider area of the mosque let alone those who went to stop him. Further to this is a likelihood of a fight breaking out. On the other hand, pouring water over the polluted area suffices and thus settles the matter. Therefore the lesser of the two evils was to let the man finish. It should be noted that the Bedouin did not urinate in the mosque with malicious intent. Rather, his action was a result of not knowing any better.

The aim in Islam is always to facilitate ease, and to be compassionate and sympathetic to the plight of human life. After all, humans are the creation of Allah, and all Allah wants is the best for His creation. The moral and ethical dilemma presented in a case where no option is left but to choose between one bad action and the other plays greatly on the human conscience. Again piety and fear of God plays a huge role in the decision making process. Evaluation of the situation requires prudence, foresight and balance. Although emotions are unavoidable these decisions require judicious thinking, reflection and cogitation. Without the fear of Allah emotions will dominate and dictate the course of action. When matters are out of the hands of people the best they can do is one with the least consequence. It is obligatory for everyone to know that Allah's mercy is the basis for His relationship with His creation, 'say to them: "Peace be upon you. Your Lord has made Mercy incumbent upon Himself ..."' (*al-An'ām* 6: 54) So let a person make difficult decisions knowing that Allah's mercy is all-encompassing.

17

The Prohibition of Causing Harm

لا ضَرَرَ ولا ضِرارَ

There is no causing harm or reciprocating harm

This maxim is, verbatim, a Prophetic tradition recorded by Imam Mālik and other hadith scholars. This hadith-turned-maxim is the authority of Maxim 9. Not only does this maxim carry great legal significance but also profound moral and ethical lessons too. As previously pointed out, one of the aims of Islamic law is to eliminate harm. However, one of the great human weaknesses, as a consequence of their predisposition of having insufficient patience, is the propensity to seek prompt retribution. This maxim acts as a legal block to prevent causing harm and reciprocating harm. Where a person has clearly made moves to cause harm to others the courts can take action to prevent it. The application of this maxim can perhaps be best seen in cases of divorce. In most cases divorce is a messy and acrimonious affair. Emotions are high and feelings are most often bruised. In such sensitively heightened cases, where the temptation to inflict harm by both parties on each other is present in abundance, the Qur'an prohibits any thought of this. Allah gives the right to the husband who has pronounced a revocable divorce to either take his wife back or release her from the bonds of marriage, but He warns the husband not to think of remaining in marriage with the intention of causing her harm: 'and when you divorce women and they have completed their waiting period, then either keep her [as your wife] in an acceptable manner or release them with good treatment. And do not keep them intending to harm them, to transgress against them.' (*al-Baqarah* 2: 231)

The ethical message plays a greater significance in this maxim than the legal role. This is because true intentions are only known by the person making it, and consequently he can always deny that his actions are intended to cause harm. Hence, the Qur'an wants to inculcate into the character of a believer that harming and reciprocating harm is not lawful. It only creates a tit-for-tat culture which is counter to the ethico-legal precepts found in the Qur'an. Islam does not teach taking revenge. However, it allows one to seek justice for the wrong done to him. It is better for a person to be patient rather than rushing to seek revenge. In seeking revenge the situation escalates and soon it gets out of control, even to the extent that future generations find themselves embroiled in petty feuds. It was for this reason that the Prophet ﷺ never retaliated against Umm Jamīlah (the wife of Abū Lahab) for throwing thorns on his pathway. The Qur'an asks us to follow the character of the Prophet ﷺ, who is described as having the best character. The Prophet's character was the Qur'an and the Qur'an instructs us: 'And not equal are the good deeds and the bad. Repel (evil) by that (deed) which is better; and thereupon, the one whom between you and him is enmity (will become) as though he was a devoted friend.' (*Fuṣṣilat* 41: 34)

18

A Principle for Prohibited Transactions

ما حَرُمَ أَخْذُهُ حَرُمَ عَطاؤُهُ

What is unlawful to take is also unlawful to give

The meaning of this maxim is quite clear and its application is easy to understand. If Islam prohibits taking something into one's possession or ownership then giving the same item is equally unlawful. Usury is an example of this. It is unlawful to take interest and therefore it is equally unlawful to give it. Both parties are guilty of an immoral crime and equally sinful, although the gravity of sin may be heavier on one party than the other. Equally, if someone is asked to deliver or keep wine in safe keeping until another person collects it from him, it is wrong and unlawful. This is because taking possession of a proscribed item is unlawful although it is only temporary. Growing poppies with the aim of harvesting opium is also considered to be unlawful. Some poppy farmers use the excuse of exporting this product to non-Muslim users, although they will never use it themselves or give it to members of their families to use. This maxim makes clear that anything which is unlawful to take is also unlawful to give. The authority of this maxim is found in the broad meaning of the verse exhorting to cooperation on piety and righteousness. (*al-Mā'idah* 5: 2) It is recorded by al-Tirmidhī, Ibn Mājah and others that the Prophet ﷺ cursed ten people regarding wine: the one who presses the grapes, and the one for whom it was pressed, the one who drinks it, the one who carries it, and the one for whom it is carried, the one who pours it and the one for whom it was poured, the seller, the one who consumes its price, the buyer and the one for whom it was bought. This hadith is clear in highlighting that prohibited actions are a two way street: both parties are sinful because it goes against the ethico-legal teachings of the Qur'an.

This maxim encapsulates the important principle of Islam to cooperate in good and avoid cooperation in vice and transgression. Rarely are sins free of victims. Either the victims are individuals, or groups of people or society. The ethical teachings of Islam do not teach only that sin has an impact on the ethico-moral-psychology of a person but also that sinful activities impact society and nations. Since evil actions often require more than two people, the responsibility therefore does not rest upon one person. That is to say, just as it is prohibited to do something, it is also prohibited to cooperate in it. Crime on a small scale can affect a few individuals or a few groups of people, and at a greater level societies and even nations are affected. Bribery is an excellent example to elucidate this point. Although in certain extreme cases where no alternative is left (and without paying bribes it would lead to loss of life or property, or dire hardship) then some scholars have allowed giving bribes, it is nevertheless an epidemic widespread in many parts of the Muslim world, corroding societies and inflicting harm on the general population and in particular the poor. It is because of this reason that both giving bribes and taking bribes have been outlawed in Islam. The ethical value Islam wants to encourage is that good must be promoted through mutual cooperation, and as a result of this people and societies will benefit.

19

A Principle for Prohibited Acts

ما حَرُمَ فِعْلُهُ حَرُمَ طَلَبُهُ

What is unlawful to do is also unlawful to request

This maxim is closely related to the previous maxim and its legal and ethical values are similar. However, in the previous maxim focus was on ownership and possession and it did not cover physical actions. This maxim aims to cover this lacuna. This maxim is simple to understand, it means that if any action is impermissible or unlawful in Islam then it is equally unlawful to ask someone else to do it. There are many examples of the application of this maxim. For instance, stealing is unlawful in Islam; therefore asking someone else to steal is equally unlawful. Both parties are sinful although the one who steals will bear a greater sin than the one who requests the theft. Likewise, murder is unlawful in Islam and therefore it is unlawful to ask another to commit murder. The authority of this maxim is similar to that of the previous maxim. That is to say, it is found in the broad meaning of the verse exhorting to cooperation on piety and righteousness. (*al-Mā'idah* 5: 2)

The ethical lesson from this has profound social and individual implications. As mentioned previously, the aim in Islam is to eliminate vice, corruption and morally reprehensible behaviour. In a case where a person has not physically committed a sin himself, by the virtue of the fact that he has requested another to do so contravenes the ethico-legal precept of cooperating on righteousness and piety. Requests to perform evil actions only promotes evil and as a result of this it causes social disorder, anarchy, unrest and unease. It is Allah Who wants the best for His creation, but discord is created due to disobedience to Allah. The Almighty says: 'Corruption has appeared throughout the land and sea due to the actions of people so Allah may let them taste part of (the consequence of) what they have done that perhaps they will return (to righteousness).' (*al-Rūm* 30: 41) The Qur'anic message is clear: only by doing good and promoting good can human society flourish and prosper. This is the natural order of life Allah has set for His creation. However, this balance is disturbed due to the corrupt actions of humankind. Therefore it is not only an obligation that one does good himself, but the obligation extends to exhorting others to do good also.

20

The Legal Significance of Custom

العادَةُ مُحَكَّمَةٌ

Customary usage is the determining factor

This is the third core maxim. One of the great signs of Allah is that He has created humankind from a single man and woman yet the human race celebrates a diverse range of colours and tongues. (*al-Rūm* 30: 22) From the design of Allah is also that He has made humans into different nations and tribes so that they may know each other. (*al-Ḥujurāt* 49: 13) It is therefore inevitable that humans will have a rich diversity of cultural heritages due to the multifarious tribal and racial connections. Culture and custom play a vital role in human life in giving a person a sense of identity and belonging, much like a person's father and mother are key to their identity and intrinsic to their social status. It is therefore no surprise that Islamic law pays much attention to custom and enshrines it as an institution worthy of regard in law. This maxim has helped jurists to stipulate and define boundaries left intentionally vague by the Lawgiver. For example, Allah commands men regarding the rights of their wives, 'Women have the same rights against their men as men have against them (*bi al-ma'rūf*).' (*al-Baqarah* 2: 228). So what are these rights? Allah commands Muslim men to live with their wives treating them with kindness, justly and fairly (*bi al-ma'rūf*). (*al-Nisā'* 4: 19) The treatment of women in terms of their auxiliary rights depends on the custom and culture of a country or area. For example, in many parts of the Western world a man would take his wife out from time to time for a romantic meal. Although this is a given expectation in Western cultures, in many parts of the Muslim world this is neither a practice nor an expectation. Therefore, a part of treating women *bi al-ma'rūf* is to live up to the cultural and customary expectation of that country. Another example of how custom is used to define Qur'anic injunctions can be seen in the precept of atoning foreswearing a vow. One of the atonements for such an offence is to feed ten paupers with 'more or less the same as you are accustomed to give to your families'. (*al-Mā'idah* 5: 89) Foodstuff and dietary habits differ from place to place, what determines this is the culture and custom of that area.

The overwhelming message this maxim is trying to give is that due respect must be extended to the culture and custom of people. Islam never came to abolish cultural practices; rather it endorsed such practices and only considered praxis that contradicted Muslim law as blameworthy and prohibited. It is important to note that it is most likely that cultural praxis has its origin in non-Islamic heritage, but continued to be practised by Muslim converts to Islam and the subsequent Muslim generations. This affirms that Islam is not culturally predatory. Culture is a ubiquitous phenomenon influencing many aspects of our daily lives. Since custom is endorsed in Muslim law and recognised it would be morally and ethically wrong to laugh and mock the cultural practice of people although some of these practices may seem peculiar to others. Rather Islam encourages everyone to look upon all cultural heritages with an open mind. The actions of the Prophet Muḥammad ﷺ are sufficient evidence, for indeed the Prophet ﷺ did not destroy the indigenous cultures and subcultures of pre-Islamic Arabia; rather he lived in harmony with them. The Prophet ﷺ only corrected those practices which came in conflict with the ethico-legal values of Islam. The Prophet's sensitivity to the cultural dialectal use of Arabic to read the Qur'an is perhaps the ultimate evidence to prove his acceptance of custom. He allowed and pleaded with Allah to permit the recitation of the Qur'an in seven popular dialectal variations. (Muslim) This was a respectful gesture towards the Arab tribes and acknowledged the integrity of each tribe's cultural identity.

21

Custom is a Legal Proof

استِعْمالُ النّاسِ حُجَّةٌ يَجِبُ العَمَلُ به

People's customary practice is legal proof and must be given regard

What constitutes custom is the practice adopted by people. These practices form and constitute a part of the law and in cases of dissention, where no instructions are found in the Book of Allah or the Sunnah of His Prophet ﷺ, custom plays a role in resolving disputes. For example, it is the customary practice in some parts of Bangladesh that a person contracting builders to do some work must also provide lunch for them. It so happened that an ethnic Bangladeshi, but a national of another country, wanted to build a holiday home in Bangladesh. Unacquainted with the customary practices of Bangladesh,[24] the contractor was shocked to learn that feeding ten builders was

24. In the province of Sylhet.

also his responsibility and a part of the contract. He refused to feed them and a dispute broke out between him and the labourers. In line with the judicial custom of Bangladesh, the case had to be referred to the village elders. The village elders were quick to pass judgement in favour of the builders.

To many living in the West this practice may seem strange. Moreover, according to Muslim contractual law it is a prerequisite that all details such as wages, conditions and pre-conditions must be stipulated prior to the agreement of the contract. Here this was clearly not the case. Technically speaking the builders were not entitled to lunch at the expense of the contractor. However, because this practice is a well-established custom in that province of Bangladesh there is no need to stipulate it, it is a known, a given without say, commonly understood and accepted amongst the people of Bangladesh. Not knowing the custom is not an excuse for non-obligation.

One of the important ethical codes Islam promotes is the cultural diversity humans have developed during their existence on earth. The aim is to harness and promote mutual respect as a higher ethical value, which will subsequently permeate all aspects of human life. One of the results of this cultural celebration is the eradication of xenophobia. During the early period of Islam, the Companions extended great respect towards the cultural practices of others.

The Hijrah, or the migration from Makkah to Madinah, illustrates how the Prophet ﷺ and the Makkan immigrant Muslims found some distinct practices in some of the commercial transactions. Islam endorsed some of these practices and only prohibited those practices which were unfair and likely to cause disputation. Hence, Islam did not seek to abolish custom, rather it sought to reform it and apply the principles of justice and equality.

22

Custom may Entail Legal Prohibition

الْمُمْتَنِعُ عادَةً كالْمُمْتَنِعِ حَقِيقَةً

What is rejected customarily is rejected in reality

This maxim is based on logic as much as it is based on jurisprudence. The maxim stipulates that if something is logically impossible to happen then no regard is paid to that claim and the courts should throw out any cases without second thought. This is because the claimant's claim is manifestly false. For example, if a woman who is post-menopausal and can no longer bear children makes a claim that a lost child is hers, it is rejected. Likewise, if a person is known to be poor and it is impossible for him to own a car yet he makes a claim that a brand new car is his. In such a case no regard is paid to his claim and it should be rejected by the courts without second thought. This is because in both cases the falsity of the claimant's claim is not only apparent without doubt but impossible too. We know the falsity of this claim without considering any evidence because customarily it is impossible for it to happen. In both these cases the judge will not listen to the evidence provided by the claimant, but reject it outright. However, it is worth noting that there may be certain cases where due to custom the judge is obliged to hear out the claim of the claimant although it is most likely to be false. For instance, if a poor man, for whom owning a brand new car is beyond his reach, claims that the car was given to him as a gift or that he won it as a prize, this warrants the judge to listen to the claim and investigate the evidence.

The ethical code in Islam is to allow everyone the right to make his claim and there is a sense of responsibility upon the judge to listen to both parties. This is an indispensable principle in Islam. It is related that the Prophet Muḥammad ﷺ said: 'Proof is required from the one who makes the claim and an oath from the one who denies it.' (al-Bayhaqī) However, Islam is a sensible religion and accepts the idea that knowledge comes from experience or perception. What provides one with this experience or perception is custom. This is because people are not born with a built-in mental content, rather their environment or culture will provide them with a cognitive faculty whereby merits of cases can be easily understood to be either a genuine claim or one not worthy of any regard. Time is precious and wasting it is a serious offence. Therefore, where there is clear-cut reason to reject a case without affording it with a hearing then it should be done so.

23

Custom has Priority over Literal Meaning

الحَقِيقَةُ تُتْرَكُ بِدَلالَةِ العادَةِ

Literality is abandoned in favour of praxis

In language, the common understanding is that the meanings of words are understood by their literal meaning. However, words can also have a metaphorical meaning. What decides whether the word is taken literally or metaphorically is the preponderant use of that word in a particular area to give the desired meaning. However, if a word is used both in its literal and metaphorical sense almost equally then preference is given to the literal meaning. The word 'idiot' was a legal term used to refer to a person who is intellectually diminished, or someone who acts in a self-defeating or significantly counterproductive way, termed in the language of

Muslim law as a *ma'tūh*. However, the term belongs to a classification system no longer in use and is now considered offensive due to the change of time. It is commonly used to insult someone and hardly any use of its literal meaning exists, whether on a societal level or in a legal context, because it is deemed to be politically incorrect. Therefore idiot cannot be taken to describe its original technical term, but rather it is considered offensive. Custom's role in resolving semantical disputes clearly shows the weight custom has in Muslim law.

Contracts, dealing and transactions are but words and it is important that the meanings of these words are understood lest dispute should later occur. It is therefore the moral and ethical code that both parties in contracts should make the terms of reference and agreement clear and beyond obscurity or multiple constructions. Humans are created with a weak disposition and suffer from being easily susceptible to corruption. Most quarrels between individuals on an inter/intra societal level are related to money and property. In many cases the terms of the contracts were left ambiguous. Disputes related to finance split societies, break up families, destroy friendships and corrode societal cohesion. This in turn violates the higher objectives of the Lawgiver of creating an environment of fraternity based on faith and fear of God or *taqwā*. Allah says in the Qur'an: 'O you who believe, be steadfast and vie in steadfastness, stand firm in your faith, and hold Allah in fear that you may attain true success'. (*Āl 'Imrān* 3: 200)

24

Only Established Custom is Considered

إنَّما تُعْتَبَرُ العادَةُ إذا اطَّرَدَتْ أو غَلَبَتْ

Custom is established when it becomes constant or a dominant practice

If regard is to be paid to custom then what becomes custom? Who decides what custom is? At what stage is a particular action considered to be custom? We know that custom is a fickle institution, ever changing due to the changing nature of the world. This maxim stipulates that for custom to constitute a valid basis for legal decisions it must be the consistent practice of a group of people. Credence is to be given to that which is publicly and generally operative and not to what is rare. Therefore, a practice to be considered as an established custom of people must fulfil two conditions:

1. The vast majority of people accept this custom. It is not sufficient for only a few people to accept it and observe it.
2. It must be a consistent practice. This means that if a practice happens due to a fad and does not have longevity then no consideration can be paid to regarding it as custom.

The application of this maxim can be seen in the case of selling a house. When a person sells a house what are the fixtures and fittings that are included in this sale without a need to mention it? In most cases it is doors, power sockets, plumbing and the like. But would curtains be included in the fixtures and fittings? The sink, taps and cabinets usually come as part of the kitchen, but does it include the cooker, oven and fridge? What would happen if these units were a part of a fitted kitchen? The answer to all these questions can be only found in the custom of people. But what happens if a person claims that he bought a house and the previous vendor sold the house with all the fixtures and fittings of a kitchen, while the proprietor of the current house has taken the cooker and oven. Does the buyer have any right to those items? In such a case, the validity of the claims can only have merit if the dominant customary practice is that the sale of a house includes all fixtures and fittings. When it becomes popular and customary then a case can be formed, otherwise these must be pre-stipulated during the agreement of sale.

Clarity is the moral case of this maxim. Clarity can either be understood as an established custom, in which case there is no need to express this in written words. An established custom is only true when it becomes the practice of the majority of people and is consistent. This is the process by which verification takes place. Verification is an important concept in Islam. Allah commands Muslims to adopt the process of verification to be a standard ethical practice for all types of information. Allah exhorts in the Qur'an: 'O believers, when a corrupt person brings you a piece of news, carefully ascertain its truth, lest you should hurt people unwittingly and thereafter regret what you did'. (*al-Ḥujurāt*, 49: 6)

25

Isolated Examples are not Considered

العِبْرَةُ للغالِبِ الشائِعِ لا للنادِرِ

Regard is paid to the dominant and widespread and not to the unwonted

This maxim is a subsidiary of the previous maxim and its shares the same ethical and moral message. The word *'ibrah* means regard is paid to or to take into consideration. This implies that there are legal consequences as a result of any consideration given to an issue. The words *ghālib* and *shā'i'* mean dominant and widespread respectively, while *nādir* means rare. These words form the integrals of this maxim. In other words, when weighing up the merits of a case which has no clear-cut guidelines in the Qur'an or Sunnah then the preponderant and pervading will be the ultimate judging factor for the case. Unlike the previous maxim, this maxim is not limited in its application to customs. Rather, it focuses on the preponderance of a phenomenon, while rare incidents although they can and do happen are ignored. For instance, let us take the modern discussions on whether it is permissible for women to travel from country to country without a *maḥram* (non-marriageable kin). The proponents of its permissibility argue that the *ratio legis* for the prohibition of women travelling alone is safety. Therefore if safety can be assured then there should be no reason why it cannot be allowed. So, if a woman is taken to the airport by a *maḥram* and received at the other end by another *maḥram* there remains no grounds for its prohibition. However, opponents to this argue that a plane can be diverted to another airport in which a woman would be stranded without a *maḥram*. While this argument may have some merit, the occurrence of this, is very rare and therefore it is not taken into consideration.

The concept of preponderance and being widespread draws its support from a Prophetic tradition which states that the Prophet Muḥammad ﷺ said: 'When water reaches a volume of two *qullah*s,[25] it cannot be affected by impurities'. (Abū Dāwūd) However, if any one of the three qualities of water (i.e. taste, smell and colour) changes due to the dominance of the impurity the water is considered impure. This implies that dominance is a factor that has weight in Muslim law.

---

25. Approximately fifty gallons.

This maxim has important applications in Muslim law. For example, bearing testimony is a duty to be carried out when requested. Anyone can be a witness provided they are upright and do not suffer from known immoral impediments. However, when it comes to giving testimony against a person's known enemy or in favour of a person's relative, it is not allowed. This is because in 'most' cases people's emotions and feelings will be a factor that influences what they will say, although in some cases this might not be true. Nevertheless, regard is paid to the dominant phenomena and not to rare isolated cases. In another example, zakat is levied on livestock which has been fed by free grazing and not on those livestock which has been fed off purchased fodder. However, if it is a combination of both then regard is paid to the dominant form of feeding for zakat to be due.

There is a great moral lesson to be taken from this maxim in terms of forming interpersonal relationships. As human beings we can err and sometimes our behaviour or statement can be influenced by a number of factors. Anyone encountering an anomalous or uncharacteristic behaviour from another person should seek to make an excuse for his brethren in faith. This is because regard is only paid to the dominant and rare incidents are ignored. If, however, a person's bad behaviour becomes the norm and a person fears influence from such behaviour reducing contact with that person can be a better thing to do.

26

Unstated Stipulations Based on Custom

المَعْروفُ عُرْفًا كالمَشْروطِ شَرْطًا

That which is known in custom is like a stipulated precondition

This maxim plays a more visible role in financial transactions. It directly highlights the significant role custom plays in financial transactions in particular and outlines the boundaries of roles and responsibilities of the contracting parties. This maxim comes into action when no verbal or written agreement has been made prior to a contract. The dispute arises afterwards and both parties make a claim against the other. In such a case custom, practice and culture will be referred to in order to judge the outcome of the case. A very good example of this can be illustrated in the following example: A man sends his son as an apprentice to learn a trade. After the apprenticeship is over both sides make a claim against the other for payment. The father claims the wages for the labour of his son and the craftsman claims payment for teaching the boy a trade. In this case, custom will judge who deserves payment.

Another example of this is going to the barber. There are two elements to this example. Traditionally and legally the price for cutting the hair must be agreed, if no agreement was made the barber is entitled to nothing and customer has received a free haircut. However, custom dictates that it is normal that no agreement is made prior to the haircut rather it is known that the barber will be paid for his service after the job is done. It is a part of the job of the barber to style a person's hair after cutting it. Therefore no argument can be made by the barber that his job is only to cut it and not style it. This is because custom has established this practice.

The ethical practice in contracts is that terms and conditions must be clearly expressed lest any dispute should arise. Honouring the terms and conditions of a contract is one of the highest moral and ethical standards in Islamic commerce. This maxim stipulates that terms and conditions which are established in custom are as good as terms and conditions expressed in words. This, therefore, equally places the responsibility of honouring unspoken terms as if they were spoken. Allah tells in the Qur'an: 'O you who believe, honour your contracts' (*al-Mā'idah* 5: 1); 'true righteousness consists in believing Allah the Last Day, the angels, the Books and the Prophets, and giving away one's property out of love of Him to one's kinsmen, the orphans, the poor and the wayfarer, and to those who ask for help ... True righteousness is attained by those who are faithful to their promise (*'ahd*) once they have made it ...' (*al-Baqarah* 2: 177) In this long list of ethical and moral precepts Allah includes the honouring of promises, which includes the promise to fulfil the terms of contracts.

27

What Custom Finds Detestable

ما يُعافُ في العاداتِ يُكْرَهُ في العِباداتِ

That which is customarily loathsome is loathsome in acts of worship

This maxim was advanced by al-Maqqarī al-Mālikī in his book *al-Qawā'id*. The maxim stipulates that if something is disliked, deemed to be repulsive or loathed by natural instinct, ordinarily or culturally then it is considered likewise in acts of worship. And just as one would avoid it naturally or culturally, one should also avoid it in matters pertaining to religion. This maxim draws its authority from a Prophetic tradition in which the Prophet Muḥammad ﷺ advised his followers: 'It is not permissible for a person to give a gift to someone and then take it back, except for a father for something he has given his son. The example of a person who gives a gift and then takes it back is like a dog that eats until it is satiated and then vomits and then licks the vomit back in.' (Muslim) The Prophet Muḥammad ﷺ disapproved of such behaviour because it is either naturally or culturally or both, distasteful to take a gift back from a person after giving it. This is with the exception of a father taking back a gift from his child, because that was seen to be culturally and naturally acceptable.

The application of this maxim can be seen in Muslim law. For example, Allah has made the entire earth a place of prayer provided it is pure. Let us suppose someone cleans the toilet area and it is now pure. Yet, it would be considered offensive (*makrūh*) to pray in that area. This is because naturally or culturally the toilet area is not a nice place. A person would not eat food in the toilet or have meetings in the toilet, similarly meeting with Allah in such an area is considered offensive. If a container is used to hold rubbish or impurities then it would be offensive to use that vessel for other purposes such as ablution, bathing or storing foodstuff. Similarly, used water is not suitable for making ablution because naturally people do not like it.

The Prophet Muḥammad ﷺ told us that he who has pride (*kibr*) in his heart cannot enter Paradise. His Companion responded, 'but a person likes to wear nice clothes and wear nice shoes', simultaneously indicating that a person takes pride in what he wears, and asking if that is considered as blameworthy pride. The Prophet ﷺ replied to the petitioner in the negative explaining: 'Indeed Allah is beautiful and loves beauty.' (Muslim) It is part of human nature to love nice things. Human beings all love to live in a nice and clean place, eat nice food, dress nicely and the like. If that is our natural instinct then the same must be observed when we are carrying out acts of worship seeking the pleasure of Allah. If anything, our attitude should be that the worship of Allah should be done whilst observing the highest standard of our expectation that we expect from others. Would it be moral as Allah's servants that we seek for ourselves that which is good but offer something substandard for Allah?

28

Certainty Takes Precedence over Doubt

اليَقينُ لا يَزولُ بالشَكِّ

Certainty is not overruled by doubt

This is the fourth core maxim. The vastness of its coverage in Islamic law and its far reaching implication led the great polymath al-Suyūṭī to assert that this maxim permeates a vast area of *fiqh* totalling up to three-fourths or more of jurisprudence.[26] What this maxim means is that something established by certainty is not dispelled or overruled by the contingent doubt. There are two elements to this maxim: *yaqīn* and *shakk*. In Arabic, certainty is called *yaqīn*. This inherently means to know something that is not tainted by any doubt. It is to have strong conviction that the state of matters is in a particular way

26. Al-Suyūṭī, *al-Ashbah wa al-Naẓā'ir*, op. cit., vol. 1, p. 115.

with no alternative possibility being the case. This conviction, of course, must be supported by reality. The antonym of *yaqīn* is *shakk* or doubt. Doubt implies the existence of an element of suspicion and uncertainty which is juxtaposed to *yaqīn*. They are two opposites, and where one exists the other cannot. Jurists have explained doubt to be in a state of indecision between the relative likelihood of two divergent possibilities. In other words a person is at midpoint, not exactly sure if it is or if it is not.

What this maxim means is that if something is certain then doubt does not affect it. For example, what would a person do if he left water in an open canister unattended for a few days, then becomes doubtful whether or not the water remains pure? In this case what is known with certainty is that the water is pure. Doubt regarding the water's purity is supervening. Therefore this supervention cannot affect something that is established with certainty.

This maxim draws its authority from Qur'anic and Prophetic sources. Allah instructs us: 'Most of them follow nothing but conjecture, but conjecture can be of no value at all against the truth.' (*Yūnus* 10: 36) The latter portion of the verse indicates that certainty cannot be replaced by doubt. Epistemologically speaking, the strength of certainty is not compatible with doubt. Therefore, doubt cannot shake the foundations of certainty. There are many Prophetic traditions which allude to the same message. It is reported that the Prophet ﷺ instructed his followers: 'If any one of you feels something in his belly and becomes doubtful (whether or not he has lost his ablution) he should not leave the mosque (i.e. his prayer) unless he has heard something or smells something.' (Muslim) This is because what is established with certainty is the fact that prayer was started with ablution. Doubt enters the person's mind after feeling rumblings in the belly. This feeling generates doubt regarding the validity of ablution. In such a case one is required to act upon certainty and dispel doubt.

This maxim has a profound impact on moral and ethical teachings in Islam. Muslims are obliged to have good opinions about others (*ḥusn al-ẓann*). This means that everybody is regarded as honest, decent and upright. Hence we know with certainty that the integrity of a person is impeccable. If that is the case, then one does not have the right to accuse someone of doing something on mere suspicion and hearsay. Allah tells us in the Qur'an: 'O you who believe avoid being excessively suspicious, for indeed some suspicion is a sin.' (*al-Ḥujurāt* 49: 12) The Prophet Muḥammad ﷺ equally warned us about suspicious conjecture: 'Beware of suspicion because suspicion is the most false of speech'. (Bukhārī)

29

The Presumption is Freedom from Liability

الأَصْلُ بَرَاءَةُ الذِّمَّةِ

The original state is freedom from liability

This maxim is one of the fundamental principles of the Islamic judicial process. Although it is a subsidiary maxim of the core maxim 'certainty is not overruled by doubt', some jurists argue that it is an independent maxim due to its far reaching application in judicial processes. There are two key words in this maxim: The word *barā'ah* means to be free of something and the word *dhimmah* means liability, commitment and responsibility. What this maxim means is that liability is a transitory and contingent attribute, and freedom from it is the original status of humans. Hence, when a person is born he is free from any liability unless proof can be provided to the contrary.

No one can possibly make a claim that a new born baby owes them money or has committed a crime against them. This state of 'non-liability' continues throughout the life of a person. Therefore a person is innocent of all liabilities, responsibilities and allegations. But if a person has a claim against another person, he must bring clear-cut evidence to prove this claim, otherwise it is rejected. The authority of this maxim can be clearly found in the Prophetic tradition where it is related that the Prophet ﷺ said if men were to be given all their claims, they would claim the blood of men and their property. Instead, evidence should be provided by the plaintiff and an oath should be made by the defendant. (see: Muslim and al-Bayhaqī)

The application of this maxim in Muslim law is vast, but some examples will help illustrate its usage. X buys something from Y. But an argument occurs about the price of a sold item after it is damaged or when it is no longer in the possession of the seller. In such a case the statement of the buyer will be considered. If Ahmad makes a claim against Zayd that he borrowed £1000, but Zayd denies this, consideration is given to Zayd's statement unless Ahmad can provide evidence to the contrary. Bakr and Umar are business partners; and their business makes a heavy loss. Umar accuses Bakr of wilful neglect and makes a claim to be indemnified. Unless Umar can bring proof to substantiate his claim, no regard is paid to his claim for compensation. In each of these cases it can be seen that favour is given to a person being free from any liabilities unless proof can be provided to the contrary.

The moral and ethical lesson from this maxim is profound. Accusations and claims against a person should not be made lightly. It can have damaging consequences on a societal level, familial level and friendships. Islam aims to foster a supreme level of fraternity and this higher objective is at danger of sabotage by making unfounded claims. If claims are to be made then let it be evidence based and irrefutable in a court of law. Otherwise, harm to a person's social standing, integrity and honour can have devastating repercussions. In equal terms, evidence should not be manufactured in order to stand in favour of any false claims. Allah Most High says in the Qur'an: 'Do not usurp one another's possessions by false means, nor proffer your possessions to the authorities so that you may sinfully and knowingly usurp a portion of another's possession.' (*al-Baqarah* 2: 188)

30

The Presumption is that Things are Lawful

الأَصْلُ فِي الأَشْيَاءِ الإِبَاحَةُ

The original rule is lawfulness

This maxim follows on from the previous maxim in trying to determine what the original state of objects is, is it a positive state or negative? Like the previous maxim positively states that man's state of origin is free from claims and liabilities, this maxim also posits a positive theme. The word *ibāḥah* means lawful and in the language of the law it denotes an action which is neither rewardable for doing nor sinful for leaving it. What this maxim implies is that everything is lawful to do unless there is textual evidence to say otherwise. For example, if it were asked, is it permissible to drive in Birmingham? The answer to that would be yes. This is because there is no textual evidence to prohibit it. If any claims are made regarding its prohibition then it is the responsibility of that person to prove it. In other words, there is no need to prove the permissibility of something through text. The fact that the text has not prohibited it is a proof of its permissibility. This maxim is primarily agreed by the Shāfiʿī jurists. Some also claim that this was the opinion of Abū Ḥanīfah and other Ḥanafī jurists such as al-Karkhī.[27]

Not all scholars agree with this maxim. Some of the *Ahl al-Ḥadīth* scholars maintain the opposite, claiming that the origin of matters is unlawfulness until proven lawful. An attempt to strike a moderate ground was advanced by some Ḥanafī jurists who asserted that the origin of matters is suspension. In other words, no ruling can be made regarding the issue until evidence is established regarding its lawfulness or unlawfulness.[28] This view seems to be impractical, because if there is evidence that the object in question is lawful or unlawful, then why would there be a need to suspend judgement? The opinion of the *Ahl al-Ḥadīth* also seems to be impractical. That is to say, to make a claim that textual evidence needs to be established stating the lawfulness of sitting on an electric sofa recliner, for example, is needed otherwise it is unlawful is absurd.

The application of the maxim 'the original rule is lawfulness' and its counter-maxims can be seen in

27. Ibn Nujaym, *al-Ashbāh*, op. cit., pp. 56-57.
28. Ibid.

many areas of Muslim law. The outcome will differ depending on the use of the maxim. For instance, in a case of eating giraffe meat those who argue that the origin is *ibāḥa* will argue that it is lawful to consume while those who maintain the opposite believe it to be unlawful. The third opinion suggests not eating giraffe until evidence can be ascertained regarding its ruling. In similar manner, the afore- mentioned three opinions can be applied to a case where a person finds a stream or pond and does not know if that is public property or privately owned. In such a case would it be lawful for him to fish in it or not?

This maxim draws its authority from a number of verses talking about halal and the haram. 'Who has made unlawful the adornment which Allah has brought forth for His creatures or the good things from among the means of sustenance' (*al-'Arāf* 7: 28); 'Do not utter falsehoods by letting your tongues declare this is halal and this is haram. (*al-Naḥl* 16: 116) These verses clearly prohibit Muslims from making vain claims of halal and haram. Rather these verses suggest that if Allah has not mentioned something as unlawful, this indicates that it is permissible.

One of the beautiful aspects of Islam is that Allah has made the lawful very easy and accommodating. The Almighty says: 'Allah wants ease and not hardship for you'. (*al-Baqarah* 2: 185) It is important to remember that the Qur'an and Sunnah bear ethico-legal values outlining the lawful and unlawful in

Islam. What is left unmentioned was not accidental but with design. It is a mercy from Allah, the Prophet Muḥammad ﷺ tells us, and warns us from probing and exploring further into it, seeking a particular ruling by extraneous unnecessary questions. (al-Dāraquṭnī) It is therefore unethical that a person insists on exploring issues that would only create hardship for himself and others. Islam is a religion of balance, perfectly marrying temporal affairs with spirituality. It is realistic in its expectations of what frail human beings can achieve. Islam only expects from the faithful real, feasible and achievable acts of worship. It considers superfluous questions as highly distasteful and causing trouble not only for the petitioner but for others too.

31

Literal Meaning Takes Precedence

الأَصْلُ فِي الكَلامِ الحَقِيقَةُ

The original rule in speech is that the literal meaning is taken

This maxim is similar to maxims previously discussed. What this maxim focuses on is how to understand what the speaker is trying to say. Human language is rich and words are powerful in what they can convey. Therefore, there are two ways in which one can understand what a person is trying to say; to wit, either its literal meaning is taken into consideration or its metaphorical meaning. Both meanings are equally valid, but how is it determined when the literal meaning is taken and when the metaphorical is taken. This maxim stipulates that all expressions must be understood in literal terms.

This is because words were originally coined to convey a particular thing. It was only later that alternative meanings were associated with some words to describe something else. Therefore, if it is agreed that an expression can have two possible understandings simultaneously; the literal meaning must take precedence over others, because the literal interpretation is the primary meaning and therefore it is certain (*yaqīn*), while the metaphorical meaning is secondary and therefore speculative (*ẓann*).

Having said this, context is an indispensable factor and the ultimate criterion to judge. Usually, the metaphorical meaning is adopted when it is not possible to take the literal. This can be due to a number of reasons, and context plays a major role in determining this. For instance, if things are said in jest or anger it can be understood in context. So when a person says, "I'm going to kill you" ... regard should be paid to context. This is because such a statement can be said in jest, anger, due to annoyance or seriously. Once context has been set, the intended meaning becomes manifest with certainty.

However, the Shariah has not made jest and anger in every circumstance free from legal consequences. It is related that the Prophet ﷺ said three things are taken seriously when meant seriously and taken seriously even though it was meant in jest: 'marriage, divorce and manumission'. (Abū Dāwūd, Tirmidhī, Ibn Mājah) The reason for this exception is to preserve the rights of others. That is to say, had not the Shariah taken these issues seriously a person could easily take it back and claim that he was joking after pronouncing divorce, marriage or vows to manumit a salve. This would leave the victims of his statements without any rights or justice.

It is important that we take care of every word that we utter. Allah tells us in the Qur'an, 'he utters not a word but there is a vigilant watcher at hand'. (*Qāf* 50: 18) Each time words are used, these have consequences because words contain instructions or convey information. Therefore it is important that a person is careful of the words he uses. The Prophet ﷺ taught his followers that the essential prerequisite for entering paradise is to watch the words one utters with his tongue. (Tirmidhī) Although words used in jokes have a very loose meaning attached to them, it nevertheless is subject to an ethical code and these codes must be observed, to wit, the joke must not contain vulgarity, offence or cause hurt. The moral message this maxim is trying to give is that when dealing with people words must be carefully selected and used to convey the exact desired meaning. Intentional ambiguity to suit one's purpose is immoral and unethical.

32

The Presumption of Continuity

الأَصْلُ بَقَاءُ مَا كَانَ عَلَىٰ مَا كَانَ

The original rule is that the status quo remains in its original state

This maxim reflects a well-known principle of Islamic jurisprudence (*uṣūl al-fiqh*) known as *istiṣḥāb*. This means that an object is considered to remain in its original state unless or until proof can be established to the contrary. This is because what is certain is the origin of the object in terms of it either being pure or impure, lawful or unlawful, doubtful or undoubtful and so forth. Therefore, unless there is evidence on the variation of the original state regard is only paid to the original state. *Istiṣḥāb* has an interesting debate in *uṣūl al-fiqh* in terms of how it is understood and applied. In essence this maxim is not dissimilar to Maxim 29: 'the original state is freedom from liability'. Hence the maxim draws its authority from similar sources. However, its main source of authority is the same as those arguments used to justify *istiṣḥāb* as a source of law. In other words it is a rational argument that presumes a degree of stability in the attributes and the nature of things. That is to say, if the known nature of something is pure then it remains pure until evidence can be provided to prove the contrary. For instance, the original state of water is purity. Therefore water in any vessel or place must be considered pure. To establish a claim to the contrary requires conclusive evidence.

Although this maxim shares similarity with Maxim 29, there is a clear and distinct difference between the two. This can be illustrated by the following examples: A husband and wife have an argument and the woman alleges that her husband divorced her. The husband, on the other hand, disputes this. In such a case, if there is no strong evidence to prove her claim then the man's statement is considered. This is because uncertainty has been introduced to a case where it is known with certainty that the marriage is valid. The superventional incident lacks strong enough evidence to counter the original state, therefore the original state is accepted to be the truth. Another example is that a person is walking along a road and accidently steps into a puddle of water. He is uncertain if the water is pure or not. In such a case a person will regard the original state of water, which is purity, unless proof is established that the water is impure.

Having a good opinion (*ḥusn al-ẓann*) is a core ethical teaching of the Prophet Muḥammad ﷺ. This maxim inculcates a positive message that the original state of things must be the way Muslims deal with worldly aspects. If one is expected to think positively about water in terms of it being pure and remaining pure, until clear evidence can be provided to prove the contrary, then the way Muslims are expected to deal with their fellow brothers and sisters is even greater. The Prophet Muḥammad ﷺ taught Muslims to always think positively about others, and make excuses for them in their shortcomings. Up to seventy excuses must be sought for a person, the Prophet Muḥammad ﷺ taught Muslims, and after that one should say that his fellow Muslim brother probably has a problem that he is unaware of. (al-Bayhaqī, *Shu'ab al-Imān*) It is by this positive attitude that Islam aims to enable society to create more love, care and thoughtfulness towards others.

33

When the Lawful and Unlawful Mix

إذا اجْتَمَعَ الحَلالُ والحَرامُ غُلِّبَ الحَرامُ

When the lawful and unlawful is mixed, the unlawful dominates

This maxim has a very pertinent and practical function in our daily lives. It is relevant today as much as it was during the early period of Islam. Some jurists argue that this maxim draws its authority directly from a Prophetic tradition because it is the verbatim reproduction of a hadith.[29] However, many scholars of hadith have criticised this tradition to be baseless.[30]

29. This was mentioned by al-Ḥāfiẓ al-ʿAjlūnī. Ibn al-Subkī also mentions this in his *al-Ashbāh* from al-Bayhaqī. However, the tradition suffers from inauthenticity due to a break in transmission (*inqiṭāʿ*).

30. See: al-Zayn al-ʿIrāqī in his annotation of *Minhāj al-Uṣūl* (See: *Khashf al-Khafā'*, vol. 2, p. 236).

Regardless of the scholastic debate whether this is a tradition or not, the meaning it conveys in terms of an ethico-legal code is deep and immense. It should be noted that this maxim is only applicable when the mixing of the lawful and the unlawful is done in such manner that it is impossible to separate the two.

The application of this maxim is very wide ranging and interesting. Here are a few examples to illustrate its application. It is known that Islam permits a Muslim man to marry a Christian or Jewish (*kitābī*) woman. All other non-Muslim women are unlawful in marriage for Muslims. If, however, a woman, is from mixed religious parents, to wit, one is a *kitābī* and the other a non-*kitābī* such as a Buddhist, Hindu or Sikh, then marriage to such a woman is not permitted unless she converts to Islam. Similarly, it would be unlawful to eat the flesh of an animal which is a crossbreed between an animal whose flesh is lawful for Muslims and an animal whose flesh is unlawful for Muslim consumption. If a Muslim and a non-Muslim work in an abattoir and the meat is mixed then all the meat in that abattoir is considered unlawful and unfit for Muslim consumption.

There is a great moral message this maxim is proclaiming and it is the cornerstone of a person's spiritual relationship with his Creator, Allah. This relationship is based on a combination of love and fear, or *taqwā*. Hence a person worships Allah because he loves Him and loves to please Him. This love is not for getting Paradise in return or any other gains, for indeed if a person worships Allah sincerely he will get Paradise and Allah's favour anyway because that is what Allah has promised. But worshipping Allah out of love means to commit to worshipping Him for no other purpose but because He is our Creator. This love should be based on the foundation of *taqwā* or the fear of Allah. Fearing someone does not mean that one does not love them, such as a child to his father. But the fear of Allah is based on the knowledge that Allah's favour upon us is so great we can never repay Him. Therefore we need His mercy and grace to overlook this shortcoming. One of the ways a person trains himself to be conscious of Allah all the time is taking the most cautious move at times of doubt. This is because he knows that by avoiding the doubtful, his relationship with Allah grows stronger, because he did this solely to please Allah.

34

Hardship Brings Ease

المَشَقَّةُ تَجْلِبُ التَّيْسِيرَ

Hardship begets ease

This is the fifth core maxim and its conceptual basis is extrapolated from the notion of *rukhṣah* or dispensation in Islamic law. *Rukhṣah* is a legal concession which the Shariah makes available in special cases. This maxim highlights Islam's concern for providing relief from hardship and its commitment to replace it with an easier rule. This is because Allah's laws are governed by His principle of 'not burdening a soul more than it can bear'. (*al-Baqarah* 2: 286) This maxim draws its authority from many Qur'anic verses and hadith. For instance, Allah declares in clear terms in the Qur'an: 'Allah wants ease for you and not hardship'. (*al-Baqarah* 2: 185) In another verse Allah tells us, 'He (Allah) has placed no hardship upon you in your religion'. (*al-Ḥajj* 22: 78) After such clear instructions from

Allah it should not be surprising that the character of the Prophet ﷺ reflects this. It is related in *Ṣaḥīḥ al-Bukhārī* on the authority of 'Ā'ishah, 'whenever the Messenger of Allah was given a choice between two things, he would choose the easier, one provided it was not a sin'. In another tradition the Prophet ﷺ instructed his followers, '... and make things easy and do not make them difficult.' (Bukhārī)

Muslim jurists have identified seven reasons which occasion dispensation (*rukhṣah*):

- Travel;
- Illness;
- Duress;
- Forgetfulness;
- Ignorance;
- Widespread affliction causing hardship to the majority (known as *'umūm al-balwā*);
- Deficiency (*naqṣ*).[31]

It is important that the term 'hardship' is qualified and understood, because it is not the intent of the Lawgiver to remove all types of 'hardship'. Waking up for the Fajr (dawn) prayer is hard and difficult, doing hajj is hard and difficult yet the Lawgiver did not provide any dispensation to not perform them. This is because the concept of worshipping Allah cannot be possible without the existence of

31. Ibn Nujaym, *al-Ashbāh*, op. cit., vol. 1, p. 7.

sacrifice, and sacrifice cannot be possible without the existence of some type of hardship. The hardship the Lawgiver wants to remove is exorbitant and unnecessary hardship which will cause harm to life, limb or property. For example, if there is no means to heat water on a cold day and a person needs to take a bath then performing *tayammum* is permissible instead of bathing. This is because it is most likely that taking a bath on a cold day with cold water will seriously harm a person if not kill him.

The application of this maxim spreads throughout many chapters of jurisprudence and Muslim law. Its significance is apparent due to its relevance in daily life. This maxim shares similarities with another core maxim 'harm is removed.' Although both have similarities and shared (and perhaps overlapping) examples and subsidiary maxims yet they are different. The notion of 'hardship' and 'harm' are similar to a certain extent yet distinct. For example, a pregnant woman who finds it difficult to fast may seek a dispensation to not fast using this maxim, while if she fears harm upon the unborn child then a dispensation is sought using the maxim 'harm is removed.'

This maxim wants to deliver a message of how a person should and ought to behave towards other people in terms of his dealings and transactions. If it is the intent of the Creator to cause and facilitate ease then it behoves that His creation emulates this behaviour.

This maxim wants to inculcate a moral message of being gentle and kind, offering compassion and helping people in difficulty. It is for this reason that Allah commands the believers to offer an extension to repay debt if the debtor is in hardship; 'and if the debtor is in straitened circumstances, let him have respite until a time of ease'. (*al-Baqarah* 2: 280) Harshness affects the heart and makes it hard while dealing with people with ease and compassion causes the heart to be soft, and to have a good hearts the true goal of Islam. Allah Most High declares: 'He who purifies (the soul) will prosper'. (*al-Shams* 91: 9)

35

Constriction Brings Ease

إذا ضاقَ الأَمْرُ اتَّسَعَ

When a matter becomes too constricted,
it is broadened

This is an interesting maxim. The full maxim reads: when a matter becomes too constricted, it is broadened and when it is too broadened, it is constricted. This means that if performing any act of worship or certain aspects of life becomes difficult then it is permissible to provide ease for people. However, once the hardship is removed the facility of providing ease is removed. This in no way means the compulsory acts of worship are subject to this maxim. For example, if the people of an area were to find the five daily prayers too difficult during the summer period but three prayers as easy then no provisions can be made to reduce the prayer. Similarly, if people were to consider giving 2.5 per cent as too much to give as zakat and wanted a lesser percentage no provisions can be made to accommodate this demand. This is because such a move will entail alteration in the law of Allah and this maxim is not to be understood as facilitating this notion. This is because the law of Allah is already moderate and Allah does not burden any soul more than it can bear. Therefore no argument can be made that 2.5 per cent is too much or five prayers are too much. Rather, the objective of this maxim is to regulate auxiliary issues and provide and facilitate ease rather than altering primary precepts. Therefore, this maxim means that if hardship requires a concession, the facility and concession is applicable in that case until the hardship ends. Once the hardship that qualifies for the facility and the concession is over, it will revert back to its original ruling.

This maxim has some interesting applications in Muslim law. For example, if a person borrows money from another person and they determine a time for its repayment, then it is a duty for the borrower to pay the money promptly. But if it happens that the borrower has fallen on hard times and requires an extension to the repayment date then that should be afforded to him. During times or places where the integrity and honesty of people have become scarce, it is valid to accept witnesses who do not fulfil the complete criteria of acting as witnesses. This is because if no concession is made then it will not let justice to be carried out and harm and discord would prevail.

This maxim has some valuable ethical and moral lessons. It is to teach and nurture the character of compassion and mercy to be an indispensable feature of a believer. Rigidity and hardship was never the *modus operandi* of the Prophet Muḥammad ﷺ. Rather, he instructed Muslims to avoid rigidity that would cause difficulty and harm (Bukhārī). The Prophet ﷺ taught gentleness and how to be gentle, deal with things with compassion, showing compassion and kindness. These ethical values are reflected in Muslim law. The Shariah is not a rigid set of laws containing harsh do's and don'ts. Rather, its main function is to regulate human life so people can live in peace and amicability. Therefore, if rigidity is found, it demands the call to broaden it until the difficulty is removed. This code of conduct should be the way Muslims behave towards their wives, children, their employees or anybody under their responsibility.

36

Benefits Bring Liability

الخَراجُ بالضَّمانِ

Benefit goes with liability

This is one of the most important maxims used in Islamic financial transactions, and has taken a central place in discussions related to contemporary financial transactions. Contemporary scholars of Islamic finance have also applied this maxim to rentals, *kafālah* (guarantee), *wakālah* (agency), *sharikah* (partnership) and *rahn* (mortgages). This maxim draws its authority directly from Prophetic tradition, because the text of the maxim is in fact a Prophetic tradition. The story behind this hadith is that a person purchased some merchandise and after few days found it to be defective. Disputing over the entitlement to a refund, they referred their case to the Prophet Muḥammad ﷺ. The seller's argument was that the buyer had used his merchandise and therefore he was not entitled to a full refund. The Prophet ﷺ, hearing both sides of the argument, decreed in favour of the buyer and told the seller, 'benefit goes with liability.' (Abū Dāwūd)

There are two words in this maxim that require explanation: *kharāj* and *ḍamān*. The word *kharāj* means return, revenue or yield. The word *ḍamān* means guarantee, responsibility or liability. What this maxim means is that the benefit of an asset is the right of the buyer. In a case where the seller sells something and fails to inform the buyer of a fault, either because he does not know of it or intentionally conceals it, the buyer has the right to return the merchandise and get a full refund even though the buyer made use of the merchandise. For example, a person sells a car. Within a few days the car exhibits major faults other than wear and tear. In such a case the buyer has the right to return the car back to the seller and demand a refund. No case can be made by the seller that the buyer used the car and therefore he is entitled to some compensation in return for using the car.

Sharikat al-wujūh is a partnership of two or more traders without capital but of good reputation. They purchase goods on credit and each partner assumes liability for a stipulated proportion of the debt created by their purchase. Their intention is to sell the purchased goods, repay the debt and split the profits. According to the Ḥanafī School, if one of the partners assumes liability for 50 per cent of the debt but stipulates 60per cent of the profits, the condition is void because his right to profits is limited to the liability he is willing to assume.[32]

It is noteworthy that this maxim only applies to the liability that comes from taking possession of an asset by ownership or by the owner's permission when the possessor takes possession for his own benefit. Therefore, a thief or a person who seizes another's property forcefully is liable for any damage that occurs to the property while in his possession and does not have any right to the yield thereof.

Responsibility is a key element in the Islamic moral and ethical code. It is related that the Prophet ﷺ said: "Each of you is a shepherd and each of you is responsible for their flock." (Bukhārī and Muslim) Together with responsibility comes honesty. Responsibility means that a person must act honestly and fairly to those under his care and to those towards whom he has a sense of responsibility. Selling merchandise comes with the responsibility that the product you are selling is free from defect and suitable for use unless otherwise stipulated. In a case where faulty products have been exchanged, the receiver of the product has the right to a refund, after all he has paid money for that product. If no provisions were made for this it would create much dispute

32. Al-Zarqā, Aḥmad ibn Muḥammad, 2001. *Sharḥ al-Qawā'id al-Fiqhiyyah*, Damascus: Dār al-Qalam, p. 430.

between people and foster hatred. Moreover, less scrupulous people would exploit this and sell faulty, substandard goods at full price in the pursuit of profit while cheating others and taking wealth on false pretences. Knowing that buyers have recourse to justice aims to mould a character of honesty and decency amongst traders.

37

Risk is Relative to Reward

الغُرْمُ بـالغُنْمِ

Liability accompanies gain

This is an interesting maxim pertinent to Islamic commercial and financial law. The word *ghurm* means loss or damage and *ghunm* means profit or gain. The meaning of this maxim is that the owner must bear all the risk and costs that attend ownership of the asset since he is entitled to enjoy any benefit resulting from it. This maxim draws its authority from the Qur'anic precept making trading lawful. (*al-Baqarah* 2: 275) That is to say, the key element of business is that it comes with risk. Investment is never free of risk. Although Islam discourages unnecessary risk taking and imprudent investment, it indicates that business investment cannot have a 'guarantee of return' stipulation. This would make it usurious. Therefore, if the business venture proves profitable the profit is shared and if it makes a loss then the investors must bear the loss.

The application of this maxim in Muslim law has many different facets and its use can be seen to be broader than the description explained above. For example, if people live in flats, then who is responsible for maintaining the communal areas such as the corridors, the lighting and cleaning of shared spaces? Since the benefits are for the owners and those living in the building, it is fair that they pay for this service. The expense for returning any borrowed asset should be paid for by the borrower, because it is he who has benefitted from its usage. Similarly, land registration fees must be borne by the buyer because he will ultimately benefit from its use. In a case of pawning, the person leaving the pawned item still has the right to benefit from it as he is still the owner, therefore he should be liable to pay for the cost of storage.

Taking risk is a natural part of life. On a daily basis we make many decisions that are based on risk. This maxim conveys a message that risk should be taken sensibly and ethically. This means greed must be avoided and halal means of risk taking should be sought. This maxim reemphasises the notion of honesty and integrity. By doing so it aims to establish fairness and equity in society.

38

The Validity of Multiple Ijtihāds

الإجتِهَادُ لا يُنقَضُ بِمِثلِهِ

Ijtihād is not invalidated by another one

This is an important maxim because it provides guidance not only to scholars but to the layperson too. The maxim means that if a jurist issues an edict on a particular issue and later another jurist hold a different view on the same matter contrary to the first one, it does not mean that the former opinion is defunct. Rather Islam allows and encourages *ijtihād*, or scholastic reasoning, on issues and it also encourages the re-examination and scrutiny of all juristic opinions. Hence any new result or verdict does not mean that the other opinion is obsolete and therefore people are not allowed to act upon it. The maxim draws its authority from the consensus of the Companions. It is narrated that Ibn al-Ṣabbāgh said that 'Umar ibn al-Khaṭṭāb gave many verdicts different to the views of Abū Bakr but never did 'Umar repeal the verdicts of Abū Bakr. It was the practice of the early Muslims that they issued fatwas on the same issues that differed from their counterparts. Examples of this can be seen in cases of inheritance where the Prophet's Companions changed their views due to other evidence. In a well-known case of inheritance, 'Umar ibn al-Khaṭṭāb passed a judgment whereby full brothers were not entitled to share with the uterine brothers a third of the deceased estate. This is based on the Qur'anic injunction that the heirs (known as the *aṣḥāb al-furūḍ*, i.e. those whose shares are prescribed in the Qur'ān) take's precedence in the distribution of the estate. In this particular case, there is no residue from the inheritance for the full-brothers as they are *'aṣabah* (agnates) and agnates will only get the residue after the shares of the *aṣḥāb al-furūḍ* have been distributed among them. However, if nothing is left after the distribution among the *aṣḥāb al-furūḍ*, agnates will not get anything from the estate. This is the gist of this case whereby the deceased left a husband, mother, uterine brothers and full brothers. According to the Holy Qur'an, the *aṣḥāb al-furūḍ* are the husband, mother and uterine brothers who are entitled to half, one sixth and uterine one third respectively. Thus, there is nothing left for the full brothers.

Later, a similar case came to light like the former one. When the case was brought to 'Umar ibn al-Khaṭṭāb, he intended to rule according to his previous judgment in the earlier case. However, one of the full-brothers raised an objection saying: 'O Amīr al-Mu'minīn! Consider that our father is a stone in the sea, isn't our mother the same? Thus how come uterine brothers inherit while we do not? Our mother is the same, and we transcend them by our father.' This made sense to 'Umar and he accepted their argument and ruled that they share a third with the uterine brothers. The grounds of 'Umar's judgment, whereby he ruled that the full brothers inherit with the uterine brothers, is that all of them are from the same mother as correctly argued by the defendants. In addition to this, full brothers have a distinction over uterine brothers as they have a stronger kinship with the deceased since they are related to him through the father as well. Hence, although their strong kinship with the deceased may not increase their portion in the estate and does not make them privileged over others, yet it shall not be allowed to disadvantage them from inheriting and from being equal to their step-brothers. When the full brothers of the former case were informed of the later judgement of 'Umar, they came and appealed to him with their objections and requested that they participate in the portion of their step-brothers according to his latest ruling. 'Umar replied with a sentence that has become a principle and maxim, 'that was our judgement and this is our judgement.'[33]

---

33. Zaydān, 'Abd al-Karīm, 2003. *Al-Wajīz fī Sharḥ al-Qawā'id al-Fiqhiyyah*, Beirut: Mu'assasah al-Risalah, p. 32.

We can see the application of this maxim to a case where a person does not know where the *qiblah* is and prayed his Ẓuhr prayer according to his guess. But at ʻAṣr prayer he changes his mind and under a revised opinion believes that the *qiblah* is in another direction and prays accordingly. This change of the direction of prayer does not invalidate his Ẓuhr prayer; even if the first direction was incorrect and the second correct.

Unity is a very important spiritual code and Allah commands Muslims to stay together. But this unity does not mean that there can be no room for a second opinion and everything has to be one single opinion. In fact Islam encourages scholarship and the scrutiny of scholastic views. But differences of opinion in juristic issues should not cause division and friction among Muslims. It is the ethico-legal precept of the Qur'an that Muslims remain united in the international arena and before its enemies. The unfortunate reality is that differences of opinion have become an excuse to differ and become divided. This maxim teaches us that difference of opinion existed in legal rulings during the best of times and will continue to do so. Therefore difference in legal rulings is on account of scholarship and not division.

39

The Subordinate Follows the Principal

التَّابِعُ تَابِعٌ

The subordinate follows the principal

This is a very interesting maxim with multiple applications in classical and contemporary life. However, the process of its application can be complicated. Further to logic and common sense, this maxim draws its authority from many Prophetic traditions. The maxim means that something attached to another thing cannot have a different legal ruling to what it is attached to. The subordinate cannot be separated from the principal. For example, if a person would like to sell a lock then the key is also a part of the lock, so no further price can be demanded for the key. This is the general rule. The subordinate can be understood in different ways:

- Intrinsic subordinate: This means that the subordinate cannot be separated from the principal; such as the organs of an animal the or branches of a tree.
- Extrinsic subordinate: This means that the subordinate can be separated from the principal; such as unripe fruits from a tree or a foetus in the womb.
- Independent subordinate: This means that the subordinate is separate from the principal; such as the key to a lock or the buttons of a shirt.
- Contingent subordinate: Such as the delivery of a purchased asset.

In each of these cases one can see how it would be difficult to separate the subordinate from the principal.

Regarding the intrinsic subordinate, there is no way to agree alternative terms, so one cannot be sold without the other, while with the second there is room for negotiation. It is narrated by Ibn 'Umar that the Prophet ﷺ said: 'If someone sells a fertilized date palm to another, its fruit belongs to the seller unless the buyer stipulates otherwise.' (Bukhārī) This is because the fertilization took place while it belonged to the seller and therefore he is entitled to it. The fruit must be in the process of becoming mature; if it is before that then the fruits belong to the buyer and it becomes an intrinsic subordinate. However, if a person were to sell a pregnant animal, the unborn animal belongs to the buyer.

Likewise, the independent subordinate cannot be negotiated and it must follow the principal, such as the key to locks or buttons to shirts or a steering wheel on a car and the like. The contingent subordinate on the other hand has room for negotiation. In a case of delivering purchased items, depending on what it is the buyer and seller can negotiate, although the primary responsibility is on the seller to deliver the goods.

Some other examples will help explain the use of this maxim. If an animal was slaughtered only to reveal a dead foetus in the womb, it is permissible to eat it. This is because the subordinate, i.e. the dead foetus, follows the principal which has been slaughtered in a lawful way. It is related that the Prophet ﷺ was once asked about it to which he replied, 'eat it if you wish, for its slaughtering occurs by the slaughtering of its mother'. (Abū Dāwūd) In zakat, the additional profit follows the principal even though a full year has not lapsed, but by virtue of it lapsing on the principal, the subordinate follows the principal.

Our children are our subordinate. The moral message this maxim is trying to get across is that it is not possible to detach your children from yourselves. Just as nobody wants to bring harm to themselves, equally they do not want to bring harm to their children. Therefore, it is important that a person not only observes good manners and offers prayer in the mosque and develops himself to be a good and decent person but also teachse these values to their children. In fact society blames the parents more than the children if they do not behave as they ought to. The responsibility of your subordinates is something answerable in front of Allah on the Day of Resurrection. Every person must therefore endeavour that they do right towards their subordinates.

40

The Proximate Cause Takes Precedence

إذا اجْتَمَعَ المُباشِرُ و المُتَسَبِّبُ يُضافُ الحُكْمُ إلىٰ المُباشِرِ

If the doer and the causer are blamed, the action is attributed to the doer

This maxim has a great role to play in criminal procedures to determine who the blame rests with and who is ultimately responsible. The meaning of this maxim is that when the direct causer of an act and the proximate causer, i.e. the person that indirectly leads to the execution of the act, come together, the ruling shall be on the direct causer as he is the foremost cause for the performance of that act. In matters of criminal procedure, in which this maxim is mostly applied, it is an indispensable value that judgment shall be based on the effective and dominant reasons not to the conducive sources. This is because the former is stronger and closer to the effect than the latter. Moreover, the act of a person who willingly and effectively intervenes between the adjacent cause and its consequential effect is the effective cause. This is because a judgement is based on the act of a willing perpetrator rather than that of the contributory circumstance.

A few examples will help elucidate the application of this maxim. If a person digs a well in the middle of a public road and someone else pushes a person or animal into the well thus causing death or injury, the person held responsible is the latter and not the person who dug the well. This is because although there is some blame on the person who dug the well, the actual cause of the act was the individual who pushed the other person or animal into the well. Therefore the blame solely belongs to him. Likewise, if a person informs another person of the possibility of stealing money and he subsequently commits the act of theft then the thief alone is held responsible and not the person who planned it for him or informed him of it. If a person is kidnapped and held hostage and a third party comes and steals his money then the blame for the theft is on the person who steals it and not on the kidnapper. It is noteworthy that although no criminal charges can be made upon that causer, this does not mean that he will not be sinful and held accountable on the Day of Resurrection or rebuked for his action; and even other criminal charges separate to the current case can be brought against him.

The moral and ethical message of this maxim can be understood from the source whence it draws its authority. Allah mentions in the Qur'an, 'Everyone will bear the consequence of what he does, and no one shall bear the burden of another.' (*al-An'ām* 6: 164) Each individual is held responsible for his own action. No claim that it was the fault of the third party can be entertained in front of Allah the Almighty. This is because Allah has blessed each individual with an intellect by which they make decisions and therefore they alone are responsible for their consequence. Taking responsibility is an important message the Qur'an and the Prophet ﷺ, teaches us. This is true in our spiritual as well as temporal life.

Index